Storage PROJECTS
for the router

Storage PROJECTS

for the router

GUILD OF MASTER CRAFTSMAN PUBLICATIONS

First published 2001 by
Guild of Master Craftsman Publications Ltd
Castle Place, 166 High Street,
Lewes, East Sussex BN7 1XU

Photographs by Anthony Bailey, with additional photographs by Stephen Hepworth
(pp 8-10) and (illustrating their own articles) by Ian Hall, Andrew Skelton, Kevin Ley,
Roger Smith, Bill Cain, Peter Barton, Peter Spiteri, Alan Parry, Terry Lawrence and
Richard Stevenson.
Illustrations by Simon Rodway, with additional drawings by Ian Hall (pp 4, 13 & 115)
and Andrew Skelton (p 10 bottom)

ISBN 1 86108 229 0

The publishers and author can accept no legal responsibility for any consequences
arising from the application of information, advice or instructions given in
this publication.

A catalogue record for this book is available from the British Library.

Cover designed by Graham Wilmott

Printed and bound by Kyodo Printing (Singapore)

contents

safety

Routing should not be a dangerous activity, provided that sensible precautions are taken to avoid unnecessary risk.

Always ensure that work is securely held in a suitable clamp or other device, and that the workplace lighting is adequate.

Keep tools sharp: blunt tools are dangerous because they require more pressure and may behave unpredictably. Store them so that you, and others, cannot touch their cutting edges accidentally.

Be particular about disposing of shavings, finishing materials, oily rags, etc., which may be a fire hazard.

Do not work when your concentration is impaired by drugs, alcohol or fatigue.

Do not remove safety guards from power tools; pay attention to electrical safety.

The safety advice in this book is intended for your guidance, but cannot cover every eventuality: the safe use of hand and power tools is the responsibility of the user. If you are unhappy with a particular technique or procedure, do not use it – there is always another way.

introduction

To be able to act on a thought or need and make our own furniture is one of the most satisfying and rewarding aspects of woodworking. The actual process of making a project may take some while, but little by little our perseverance brings dividends and the item evolves before our very eyes into something to be cherished. We all have an innate need to change our immediate environment – to personalise it – and woodworking is one area in which we can bring this about.

In recent years there has been a massive increase in the number of people taking up woodworking, and this has resulted in an insatiable quest for knowledge about the tools, equipment and methods of creating things. The router is one of the most widely used pieces of woodworking equipment. It is without doubt, the most versatile piece of woodworking equipment currently available and, remarkably, is the only one to have spawned its own defined culture.

Not only is it fast, accurate and capable of being set up in only a few moments, but the wide array of accessories and jigs available means that it can be used for profiling, detailing, moulding, rebating, and creating simple and complex construction joints a-plenty. In fact, it is impossible to list everything that a router is capable of doing. One thing is certain, however: when you have used one for a number of years it is difficult to imagine woodworking without it.

Some of the most widely tackled projects are connected with storage. No matter what size our house or workshop may be, we all discover sooner or later that we lack sufficient space to store all of our bits and pieces. Two truths of routing are that necessity is the mother of invention and that no two situations can be tackled in the same way – which is why this book has been created.

Router users are by default inventive and lateral thinkers, finding ways to overcome problems by creating jigs and accessories to tackle the job in hand, and this book brings together the best of the projects on storage featured in *The Router* magazine. Each features a clear step-by-step commentary on its creation, together with practical hints and tips on creating jigs and how to get the best out of your router.

Although you will close the book fully equipped to produce a wide range of handsome projects (as many as two dozen in all), the imaginative ideas included in their making will almost certainly stimulate you to improvise yourself. Andrew Skelton's wheeze of using different timbers for his school shelves, with the names of each carved in the wood as an educational aid, could easily be adapted in some way for one of your own projects, while the box replica of the island of St Michel dreamed up by Terry Lawrence invites a similar ingenuity in crafting small storage vessels to resemble favourite places of your own. As for materials, Kevin Ley's attractive desk in fumed mahogany and burr elm is a reminder that not everything has to be made of oak, ash or pine, useful and versatile as those timbers are.

Those of us who manage to spend almost as much time in the workshop as in the home know how important it is to be organised when you are routing, and several of the later projects in the book are ideal for keeping things in order. Tidiness, after all, is closely allied to safety, and

containers for routers, cutters and other tools are therefore more than a luxury. As with the items for the home, the makers of these workshop projects have spent years at their craft and know how important it is to fashion things which not only function perfectly but which are enjoyable to live with.

Their enthusiasm in infectious. Whether you are looking to create a stunning shelving display for the dining room, or a wall unit for the workshop, I guarantee that you will have fun working through the projects in this book.

Mark Baker
Group Editor, Woodworking
Magazines, GMC Publications

STACKED to perfection

Ian Hall finds a home for a mountain of books

After one of our old bedrooms was converted into an office containing an ever increasing mountain of books (courtesy of my wife's college course), there came about a desperate need for a large bookcase which I could see fitting on an invitingly vacant wall. From the outset I decided that it was to be a self-contained, open-backed unit needing minimal wall fixings and, because of its great length, it would have an in-built cure for the inevitable shelf sag.

"If you already have the full width boarding, then the piece could be knocked up on a wet Wednesday afternoon..."

NO SAG HERE

It is an extremely simple design utilising a rear central muntin notched through each shelf with a pair of dividers. These have been added primarily to counter the sag and allow a full width of run on the second shelf. There is plenty of scope here for the biscuit jointer. However, the sides were asking for through tenons to show off some wedges to brighten up an otherwise rather plain piece.

Four fillets were added to the outer corners to provide hanging points as well as giving a little stability for handling. With these drilled to take No. 12 screws and a fifth screw hole added through the muntin, the whole assembly becomes extremely sturdy. If you already have the full-width boarding, then the piece could be knocked up on a wet Wednesday afternoon, but my case involved most of Tuesday collecting, thicknessing and joining up the boards.

CONSTRUCTION

Gauging from the back, the tenon-spacing is deliberately equal regardless of shelf width, so that the four shelves can be clamped together. Here, the router is best utilised machining tenons in with the use of guides clamped

Photo 1 Bracket shape for wall hanging

Photo 2 Neat but efficient padauk wedges

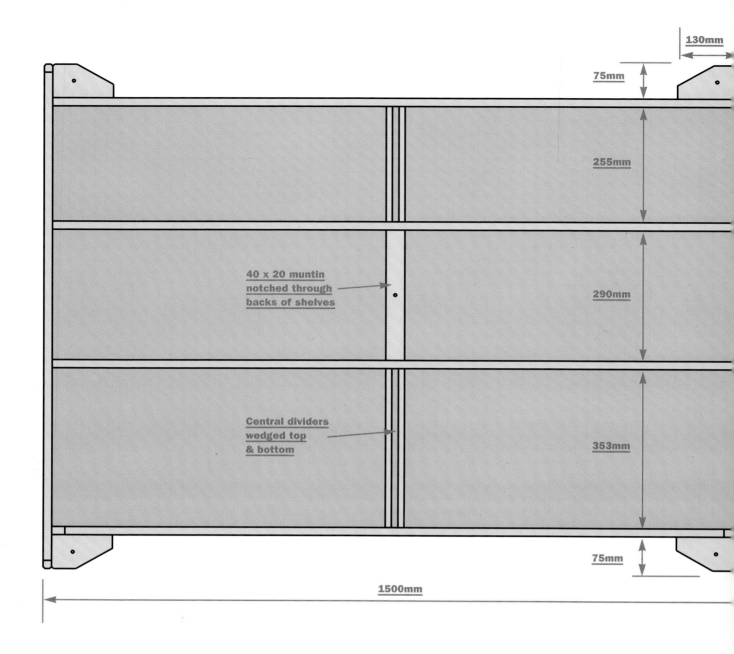

130mm

75mm

255mm

40 x 20 muntin
notched through
backs of shelves

290mm

Central dividers
wedged top
& bottom

353mm

75mm

1500mm

across the ends.

Give yourself 1 or 2mm of tenon depth while setting the router for flushing off after assembly. The tenons can then be marked down directly onto the side-cheeks and the mortices chopped. A dry assembly now gives the best dimensions for the muntin and dividers which are similarly produced as the shelves.

Once the muntin is dimensioned, it can be notched through all the shelves, then plan the dividers to butt against this and eventually to be screwed through from the back of the muntin. I used the tenon saw to produce the fox-wedge slots to the full depth of the tenons and was careful to cut them the right way!

I made the wedges from padauk by producing a strip about 3.5mm (9/64in) thick by the width of tenon, then by progressively sharpening the tip to a taper as a guide-in: they can be chopped off to the required length with perhaps a few to spare. Simple 6mm (1/4in) stopped slots

were routed into the fitted shelves, side-cheeks, corner blocks and loose tenons made of ply to give mechanical strength to this area. Remember that the bookcase is capable of carrying enormous weight.

FINAL ASSEMBLY

I had a complete dry run of the assembly followed by a 'wet-run' using Cascamite and gave myself plenty of time for knocking in all those wedges. Fox-wedging is a one-way trip, being unforgiving of silly mistakes. When fully dry, sand well to flush the protruding tenons and wipe over quickly with white spirit to find any glue spots.

My example shows a simple antique stain followed by a good quality polish which matched the furnishings of the room. With the five holes drilled to suit my now polished round-head screws, the unit was ready to hang.

"I used the tenon saw to produce the fox-wedge slots to the full depth of the tenons and was careful to cut them the right way!"

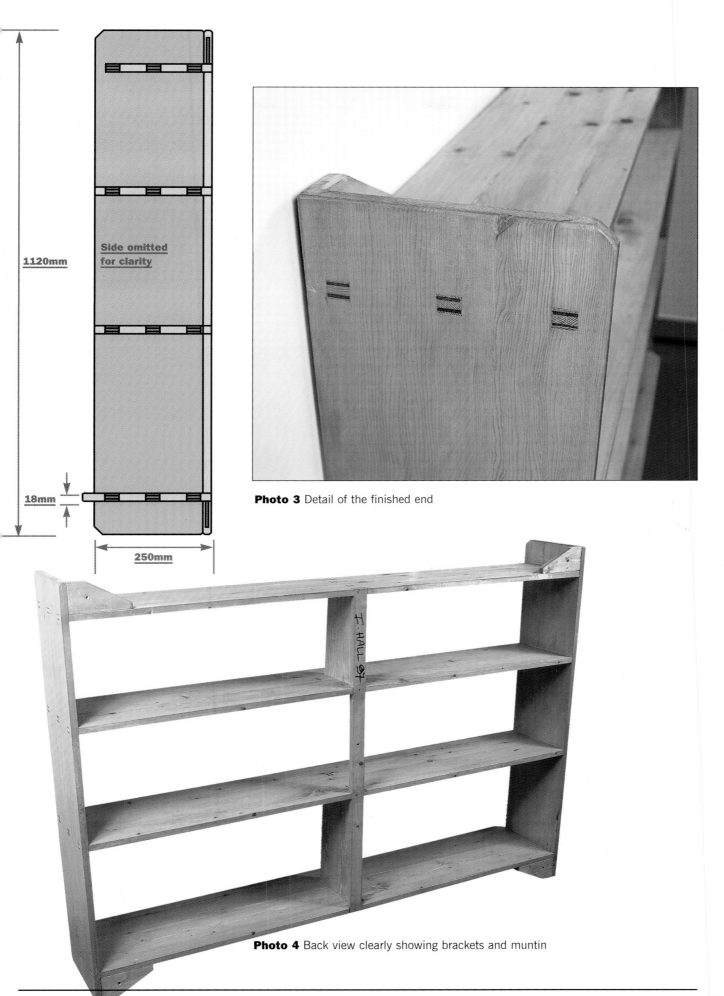

1120mm

Side omitted
for clarity

18mm

250mm

Photo 3 Detail of the finished end

Photo 4 Back view clearly showing brackets and muntin

School

Andrew Skelton

Andrew Skelton on building
education and quality into
budget-priced shelving

report

I WAS delighted when the local
primary school, at which I have three
children, asked me to make some
shelves for them. They had to fit in a
space, hold a certain number of books and
be made to a price.

My design uses a minimum amount of
material and a quick, conventional form
of construction.

The design
The shelves were to be made up of three
units which go either side and beneath an
existing notice board and fit over a heating
pipe, *see fig 1*.

I came up with the idea of using different
timbers for the shelf lippings into which the
names of the woods are carved.

They had to fit on a wall which varied by
about 20mm (¾in). Thus the carcass is
rebated by 6mm (¼in) for the back plus a
20mm (¾in) allowance for scribing to the
wall, making the sides and top 26mm (1in)
wider than the shelves, *see fig 2*.

Cutting MDF
MDF was chosen for its ease of use and
ready-to-finish surface. Unless the shelves
are to be fixed and screwed through the back
they must be 25mm (1in) thick for spans of
600mm (24in) or more. This is to avoid sagging when the shelves are loaded.

Once the pieces are cut to width they can
be left over length, the edges being carefully
shot on the overhand planer for lipping.

Gluing lippings
The lippings are prepared a touch oversize
and biscuit slots cut every 100mm (4in) or
so. When gluing the lippings use an adhesive
with a long open time and cramp up the
lipped shelves two or four at a time, arranging the pieces in the cramps lipping-to-lip-
ping so that the width of the MDF distributes
the pressure evenly, *see photo 1*.

When the glue is set, clean the lippings
flush with a sharp plane or belt sander and
cut the pieces to length.

▲ *Photo 1 – Cramping up lippings in multiples.*

Cutting mitres
Trim the long mitres with a router fitted
with a 45° cutter capable of chamfering a
25mm (1in) board.

The cutter's guide bearing follows an
MDF straight edge clamped to the underside of the piece being mitred. This straight
edge should be about 30mm (1¼in) wider
than the mitre at each side to allow a safe

lead in, and a scrap piece screwed to it prevents the lipping spelching out at the end of
the cut, *see photo 2*.

Biscuit joints
The biscuit slots can now be cut, a router
fitted with a slotting cutter will achieve this
easily. Handle with care until the biscuited
butt joint can be strengthened by the back.

▲Photo 2 – Routing mitres: cutter looks lethal but works well, note anti-spelch fence screwed to guide board.

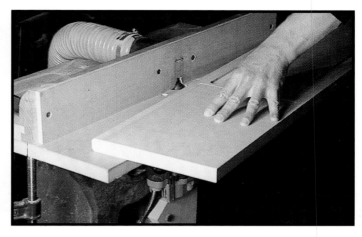

▲Photo 3 – Lippings are chamfered on a router table

Photo 4 – Corner detail showing chamfered mitre ▼

"Whichever adjustable shelf support system is chosen the holes will never be in the right place"

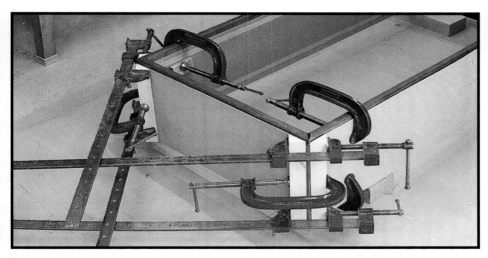

▲ Photo 5 – Use of the mitre clamping blocks

Use a scrap of MDF, marked with the position of the biscuits, clamped to the uprights as a fence for biscuiting, the same piece can be used to position the fixed shelves.

A mitred biscuit joint seems to be strong, but be sure to set biscuit slot towards the inside of the mitre where it has the most bulk. A mitre in 25mm (1in) material will take a No. 20 biscuit.

Chamfers

There are many methods of supporting adjustable shelves, from drilling scores of holes to using ready made systems – whichever is chosen, the holes will never be in the right place! If using a tonk strip which is set flush with the surface, rout the channels for it at this stage. Next rout the rebate on the back edge, and attend to the chamfers, see photo 3.

These run through all the joints, and the ends of the fixed shelves and mitres are chamfered with a chisel.

I chose to do this to emphasise the inter-sections of the pieces and show clearly that some joints are at 90° and some at 45°; usual practice would be to make the joining as perfect and invisible as possible.

Staining lippings

This approach also allowed the staining and finishing of each component before assembly; the giant size 'Danish shoulder' hides any slight misalignment.

The lippings can be stained after the edges and chamfers are cleaned up. I used a water stain so it was necessary to raise the grain and sand back several times before application.

To stain only the lippings leaving the MDF clean, apply as carefully as possible; when it is dry rout a 1.5mm (¹⁄₁₆in) V-groove to clean up the ragged edge, see photo 4. With all the joints masked the components can be finished with a hard-wearing lacquer.

Dust protection

Cutting MDF is a heavy and unpleasant task, and precautions must be taken against the dust produced. This dust presents a serious health hazard, so dust protection capable of filtering sub-one micron particles must be worn. Budget dust masks do not qualify – use only those for which the makers provide specifications of protection levels, and for sustained use choose an air-fed respirator.

Remember that the dust remains suspended in the air for some time after machining.

Carcass assembly

Triangular blocks, glued and screwed to hardboard or thin MDF, are G-cramped tightly to the carcass. The mitres are drawn together with cramps applied to these blocks; in this way the pressure acts directly across the joints, *see photo 5*.

The lower joint is cramped with sash cramps top and bottom, using slightly rounded blocks to apply pressure over the whole width. Glue can easily be wiped off the finished surfaces, another benefit of finishing before assembly, *see photo 6*.

The back is cut from 6mm (¼in) MDF and lots of small fixings were used to spread the load and create a strong structure. No. 4 screws were inserted every 150mm (6in or so) – note that while No. 6 screws into the endgrain of 25mm (1in) MDF might work, No. 8's will almost certainly cause the material to delaminate.

Carving names

I am no carver and have only a few gouges picked up in second-hand shops, but I would recommend anyone to attempt carving the names. The letters can be printed out from a computer at the appropriate size and traced through using carbon paper, or marked out using Letraset-type rub-down transfers.

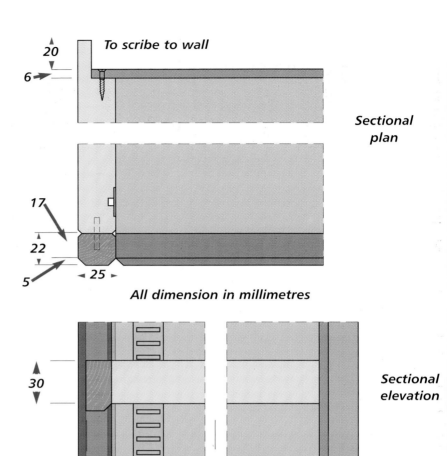

To scribe to wall

20

6

Sectional plan

17

22

5

25

All dimension in millimetres

30

240

Shelf width

Sectional elevation

Fig 1

▼ *Photo 6 – Lower joint cramped with sash cramps and slightly curved blocks*

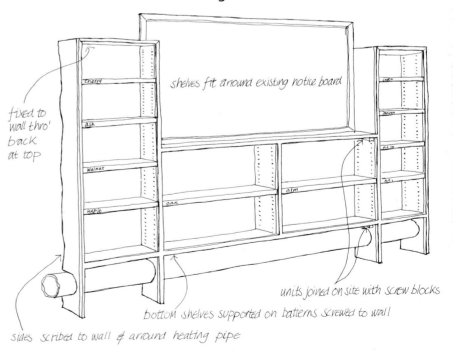

shelves fit around existing notice board

cherry

ash

walnut

maple

oak

elm

fixed to wall thro' back at top

units joined on site with screw blocks

bottom shelves supported on battens screwed to wall

sides scribed to wall & around heating pipe

Fig 2

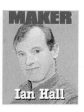
MAKER
Ian Hall

Tidy tech

Ian Hall routs an ingenious computer cabinet which will tidy up the technology in your home

SEVERAL years ago our long-awaited computer arrived. As it was being assembled and its various parts were deposited around the dining room I suddenly realised how little thought had been given to where exactly the thing was going to live!

As the kids took to it like riding bicycles, they were totally oblivious of the 'birds-nest' of wires which may be intrinsic in an office, but not in my dining room.

Planning

I was immediately driven to the drawing board with a determination to house every-thing in one unit. I soon realised the ergonomics involved were similar to that of a bureau's writing height concerning the keyboard, but a fall flap wouldn't work and where could I put the mouse mat?

At this point the engineer in me mani-fested itself, so I decided on a sliding shelf which operated telescopic wooden mechanisms each side. The printer sits on a similar shelf that slides, at a lower level, to gain access for paper loading, and I felt a drawer was essential.

I wanted a single plug to supply the cabinet, so some sockets were to be built in. When I spotted that the operating switch for the printer was at its back, a remote switch at an upper level seemed a good idea.

The mouse-mat problem was solved by utilising the folding flap stay from an old kitchen table, allowing the mouse-mat flap to swing below the keyboard shelf, but this involved a lot of fancy engineering – definitely a one-off.

A cabinet was soon knocked up in soft-wood and is in daily use, mainly by teenagers, which stands testament to the sliding shelf design and provides a useful proto-type for the much improved version before us now.

▼**This beautiful cabinet hides a secret within... it opens up to reveal a useful but unsightly computer**

First, make up the plinth and rout the housings for the carcass sides

Select and machine the five parts that make up the monitor shelf

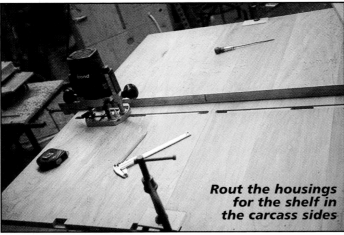

Rout the housings for the shelf in the carcass sides

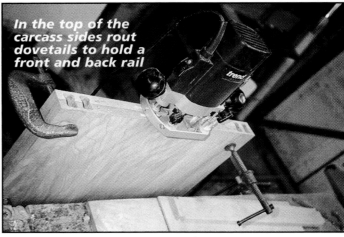

In the top of the carcass sides rout dovetails to hold a front and back rail

This version will take a 15in monitor and tower, has discreet wiring for the remote printer switch and features both right and left-hand mouse-mats. Many thanks to Editor, Alan Goodsell, for the latter attribute, as he once said to me, and I quote "what about left-handed buggers like me?".

The drawings show the exact dimensions of my cabinet which, of course, may be altered to suit your own equipment.

Carcass

Obviously, a decent scale drawing of the whole piece is a must, and I also did a full-scale one of the sliding movement, fully open and closed.

The carcass above the monitor shelf is completely backless, mainly for the circulation of air (essential for computers), but also to give easy access to the connections.

Rigidity of carcass is achieved by two panels of 6mm ply on its back, the lower rising from the plinth to just above the printer shelf, the other dropping from the monitor shelf to just below the keyboard shelf, which is removable for gaining access.

Being removable it must be fitted flush, so I fitted the lower panel similarly but glued and screwed to maximise rigidity.

Plinth

Start with the plinth, a 64 by 34mm section which has mitres to the front, jointed with

Cut the feet to shape and secure in place (believe it or not the scroll-saw in the background was actually made by the author – Ed)

Dry fit all the carcass components together to make sure they fit

▲ *Cutaway drawing clearly shows how the cabinet is made*

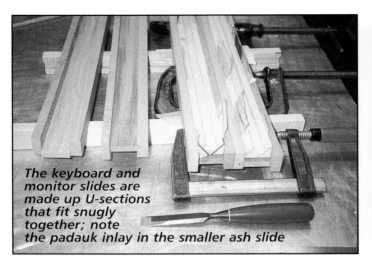

The keyboard and monitor slides are made up U-sections that fit snugly together; note the padauk inlay in the smaller ash slide

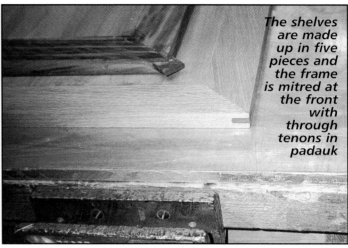

The shelves are made up in five pieces and the frame is mitred at the front with through tenons in padauk

▲ Wide, shallow housings are routed into the carcass sides to take the shelf slides

loose tenons and a rear cross-rail. Once assembled it can be squared precisely to ensure that the sides are parallel. The router will follow these when trenching out the slots for side cheeks.

I usually run in a slot underside for locating feet at this stage, and the ogee moulding around the front and sides completes the base.

Board up for the carcass sides to suit plinth slots, followed by the three top rails using dovetails on all, the top being simply planted on these and screwed without glue.

Shelf

The shelf is made up from five components. Front, rear and middle rails are morticed and tenoned into side cheeks. The two remaining parts, which are basically panels, are tongue and grooved into rails, leaving a little slack for natural movement, and housed just 3mm deep, with no use of glue, into the sides. Mark out the inside of the carcass sides exactly where the shelf is to go and rout the housings.

Make and fit two rear rails, which take the 6mm ply backs and the single rail to the front, above the drawer which acts mainly as a door stop.

I decided that the sliding mechanism must logically come next so that each could be fitted individually to the inside cheeks. I used oak (*Quercus robur*) for the housings, ash (*Fraximus excelsior*) for the telescopic sliders and oak again which lips all round the sides of the shelves.

The diagram shows the dimensions to which I worked, and although the back of main housings appears a little thin, they are deeply set in side cheeks, glued to the front and slot screwed at the back, making them very strong.

Letting in

The lower section of the slide housings which carry the printer-shelf act as kickers for the drawer and therefore match the section of cross rail above drawer.

Each U-section is made from three parts to control grain-flow, and I decided to strengthen the front ends of the ash sliders by inserting ornate loose tenons in padauk (*Pterocarpus soyauxii*) as a feature.

I wanted the sliding shelves to be as stable as possible, so I opted for veneered panels, lipped all round with oak with mitres to the front, jointed with through tenons in padauk, again a feature.

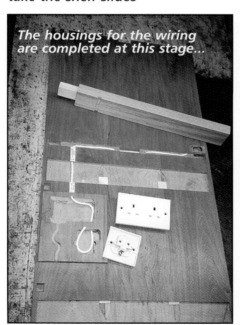

The housings for the wiring are completed at this stage...

... then the electrical fittings are installed along with the shelf slides, a coat of Danish oil is easier at this stage too

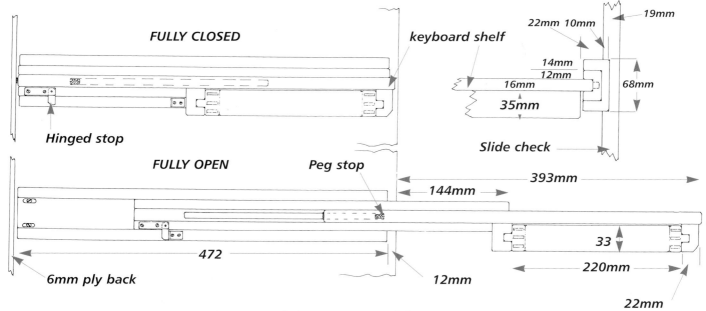

FULLY CLOSED

keyboard shelf

22mm 10mm

19mm

14mm
12mm
16mm

35mm

68mm

Slide check

Hinged stop

FULLY OPEN

Peg stop

393mm

144mm

472

6mm ply back

12mm

33

220mm

22mm

▲ Cutaway of the computer cabinet

When the carcass is assembled rout the
rebates for the plywood backs

The shelves are finished to 16mm
thickness but left several millimetres oversize all round until final fitting.

The router comes into its own at the next
stage when 'letting in' the slider housings
and electrical gear. At this point I wished I'd
made Roy Sutton's housing jig! *See TR 2.*

I managed at this stage to 'lose' the wire
that supplies the remote printer switch
through the monitor shelf joints and
behind the slider housing, down to its
printer socket. Remember to take the
advice of a qualified electrician before
embarking on the electrical work.

With the insides nicely exposed and
housings assembled I applied Danish oil to
all exposed areas above the drawer as this
would be difficult after gluing up. I also
added the row of telephone clips which will
support the mouse-mat and keyboard cables.

After a dry run the carcass can be glued up
– the side cheeks being glued and screwed
only about 75mm to the front of the channel
in the plinth and slot screwed at the back.

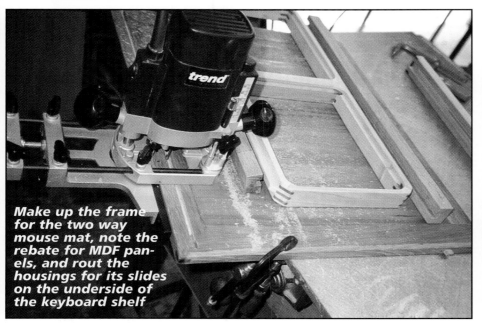

Make up the frame
for the two way
mouse mat, note the
rebate for MDF pan-
els, and rout the
housings for its slides
on the underside of
the keyboard shelf

The drawer is constructed
using dovetails, and housings
are made for the internal
compartments

A large cove cutter creates recesses in the drawer front for getting fingers in

The conventionally constructed doors have a stopped chamfer feature

Rebates

The rebates to take the backs can be run in now. Plan robust fitting of the ply as the panels act as stops for the sliding shelves. It is important not to finally fit the lower back panel as access is needed to fit the sliding shelves, but lightly fitted will give rigidity for safety. With the feet glued on I usually give the entire underside a coat of finish.

With the ash sliders in place the shelves can be fitted in width, trimming equally each side so that mitres come correct when trimming for finished depth.

I planned a 3mm clearance to the doors and a strip of rubber bonded on the back of the shelf softens the stop. The shelf has a peg each side which picks up the middle slider via a slot of pre-determined length.

This whole assembly is brought to a halt against further stops which I machined from duralium and are positioned externally. They feature one half having a rubber pad shock absorber, the other half having a hinged part so that the whole business can be withdrawn for regular waxing of movement.

The proto-type has non-removable sliders and has now lost its original smoothness due not only to lack of waxing, but also to ingestion of uninvited debris. Had I not been an engineer the stops would have been made in hardwood.

Mouse-mat platform

The platform actually utilises two mats, and I designed a left and right-hand action under-slung at the front of the keyboard shelf. Its two main jobs are to fit between the ash sliders when closed and to clear their fronts when fully deployed.

At the design stage two standard mats were placed on the full-scale plan and the platform literally drawn around them. It is basically a mitred frame, again using padauk loose tennons as a feature, heavily chamfered on the corners with tongues routed on the sides.

The front guide is glued and screwed, but the rear guide is just screwed to give a little adjustment when finally fitting. The length of slots and the positions of stops within the sliding shelf action are largely governed by the final position of the platform.

▼ **Round the back the plywood strengthening panels can be seen**

▼ **A peek inside shows the drawer partitions**

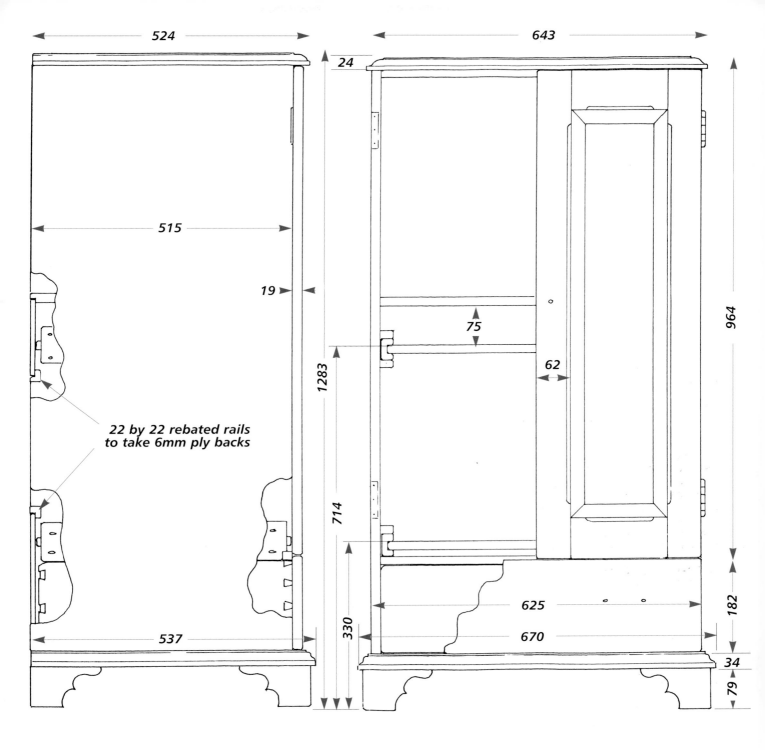

▲ Dimensions, in millimetres, of the computer cabinet

Drawers

The drawer is completely conventional, except that I provided pockets to the front for storing CD's. These are an elaborate affair using 6mm solid sections which took lots of time.

The action of the drawer was raised slightly by gluing some 2mm strips to the insides of the plinth, thereby preventing the drawer from scraping across the top of plinth. With the drawer fitted satisfactorily, its front can be positioned and fixed.

Doors

The doors are completely conventional in build. An earlier prototype I made has a single door which, apart from having a

frighteningly large swing, doesn't give the cabinet a balanced appearance, and I think a pair look much better.

I've used magnetic catches but fitted them unconventionally. I broke up the catches to retrieve the magnetic bits, then buried them in the front of the monitor shelf with about 1mm protruding, pinning them from beneath.

The catch plates were set into the doors and luckily the knobs worked out at the same level so I was able to hide the heads of the knob screws beneath the catch plates.

I particularly enjoy setting out and hinging doors, and the router is a priceless tool for me here.

Because I intend to show the cabinet I polished and lacquered the brass fittings.

Finishing

I hate not being able to wax up the moving parts immediately after they're made, because the piece is waiting for a finish. I applied many-many coats of Danish oil, cut back every couple of coats with ever-finer paper until 0000 wirewool was used.

I also employed my trusty old sable brush because a paintbrush, at best, will give a paintbrush finish! Keep the top separate to avoid having to work under the overhang.

Burnishing paste brought it to the finish I required, and with the top screwed on and all moving parts waxed, a very enjoyable task was brought to a conclusion.

FUMING

Kevin Ley makes a desk in fumed mahogany and burr elm

The last order I was able to make in my old workshop was for a tall, tapered chest and companion desk with a single, tapered, three drawer pedestal. The client had seen my burr elm apothecary's chest in an exhibition in the Bowes Museum. When he came to buy it, he enquired about having a small desk and chest of drawers made. Fortunately, I had an oak tapered pedestal desk in the house which I had just completed for another client. When he saw it he was taken with the idea of the tapering pedestal, and decided to have one for his desk. He then saw a tall shaker style chest I had made some time ago, and, drawing it up on the computer to get a sense of the proportions, he decided, albeit a bit nervously, to use the taper for this companion chest of drawers in order to have two matching pieces.

wild, wild wood

My client was very keen on the burr elm, not only because of its beautiful figure, but because it was gathered locally from the hedgerows where elms have all but disappeared. However, we quickly realised that to make the whole piece from burr would be highly impractical. Firstly, I did not have enough burr or the sizes required, and secondly it was unsuitable for most parts of the construction. Although wild grain gives the piece its stunning figure it has the drawback of lacking stability and strength and is prone to being somewhat 'unpredicatable' when worked.

The final decision was to use a relatively small amount of burr but to maximise its impact by using it for the drawer fronts. The remainder of the carcass construction was to be made from fumed, oiled Brazilian mahogany to provide a contrast of colour and figure while also emphasising the burr and giving a richness to the finished piece. Fuming immediately brings out the deep red colour of the mahogany, usually only reached after some time. As the chest was to be used for clothes storage, we opted for cedar of Lebanon, with its distinctive pleasant smell and insect repellent properties, for the drawer casings.

The Brazilian mahogany with its relative lack of figure, consistent grain and absence of faults, was easily selected, cut and dressed oversize and then stacked with separating sticks and placed in the conditioning cabinet. The cedar of Lebanon

for the drawer casings was treated likewise, with this stack weighted on the top.

Selecting the burr was much more demanding. The surfaces had to be examined carefully for figure, colour and faults. Then the provisionally chosen pieces were marked with chalk and put together to gain an idea of the overall effect. Next they were cut oversize, faced, thicknessed, checked again, then wiped with white spirit to show an approximation of the finished colour. After a final examination in detail, the pieces were clearly marked, stacked, sticked, weighted on top, and placed in the conditioning cabinet for a few days. The mahogany was removed to begin the project while the drawer material was left in for as long as possible.

carcass construction

The carcass construction was fairly standard with the sides housed directly in to the top, and the drawer frames housed into the sides. The complication was in the taper. To make the measurements of distances and angles easier, it was essential to draw the front of the chest, full size, on to a piece of hardboard. Next, I

transferred the angle of the sides from the vertical, as accurately as possible, onto a suitable piece of plastic (although hardboard will do) about 100mm (4in) square, and then cut it and used it as a reference for all machine settings and angle cuts for the piece.

taking sides

First the sides were made up using two widths of mahogany for each one. The figure was matched carefully and the joint strengthened with a ply loose tongue. A 9.5 mm (3/8in) deep x 5mm (3/16in) wide slot was cut in the sides and top for the back, taking care to stop the slot in the top short of the overhang.

Next the housings for the drawer frames were cut. With the exception of the top and bottom, these housings were 19mm (3/4in) wide x 9.5mm (3/8in) deep (at the shallowest side) to take the full thickness of the frames. The top frame housing was 9.5mm (3/8in) wide and offset down to avoid the tenon for the top. The bottom housing was also 9.5mm (3/8in) and offset up, to leave room for the cut out to form the side feet (**Figs 1&2**).

All the housings were cut at the required angle

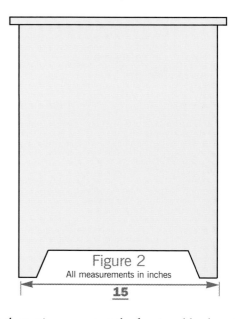

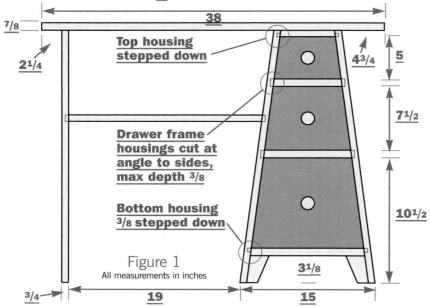

Photo 7 Using base block while cutting housing **Photo 8** Cramping to ensure even pressure

Figure 1 — Top housing stepped down; Drawer frame housings cut at angle to sides, max depth 3/8; Bottom housing 3/8 stepped down. Measurements: 38, 7/8, 2 1/4, 4 3/4, 5, 7 1/2, 10 1/2, 3 1/8, 3/4, 19, 15. All measurements in inches

Figure 2 — 15. All measurements in inches

by fixing a block onto the router base to raise one side. The ends were then chiselled square and the housings cleaned out carefully.

in the frame

The frames were made up from 50mm (2in) x 19mm (3/4in) mahogany, with the sides tenoned into mortices in the front and back rails. The back rails were made 1mm longer than those on the front to make for an easier drawer fitting and running. The front joint was glued, the rear joint dry fitted and an expansion gap left to allow for subsequent movement, (**Fig 3**).

The shoulders of the frames were marked on the front and back with the angle marker, 9.5mm (3/8in) in on the bottom edge and cut 9.5mm (3/8in) deep with a tenon saw. The top and bottom frames were also rebated to 9.5mm (3/8in) and all of them were individually dry fitted and finished.

Housings for the front feet were cut 6mm (1/4in) deep on the front of the sides and the bottom frame. The feet were cut to size, dry fitted and finished. Cut outs for the feet on the sides were made and the edges finished. The angled shoulders on the top of the sides (where they fit

in to the top), were cut at the front and back and then finished.

The top was made up from three widths of 19mm (3/4in) mahogany. As with the sides, the figure was carefully matched and the joints were strengthened with a ply loose tongue. Care was taken to stop the slot for this tongue well short of the edge, so that it was not exposed when the edge was chamfered. Next the angled housings in the top, to take the sides, were cut. This was done in the same way as the angled housings in the sides, which were dry fitted to the top to check for a good joint. These housings were 1mm further apart at the back, to correspond with the extra length of the back of the frames.

The chamfer on the underside of the top was then marked, and a strip of wood was clamped to the top, in the relevant place as a fence. A sharp jack plane was used to remove the bulk of the waste. The plane was sharpened, reset fine, and the final light finishing cut was made. A light sanding finished the job.

The back was made from 5mm (3/16in) mahogany faced MDF. I intended to use it as a brace during the assembly and gluing up, to help keep the shape of the carcass. It was cut

Assembly had to be approached with even more care than usual

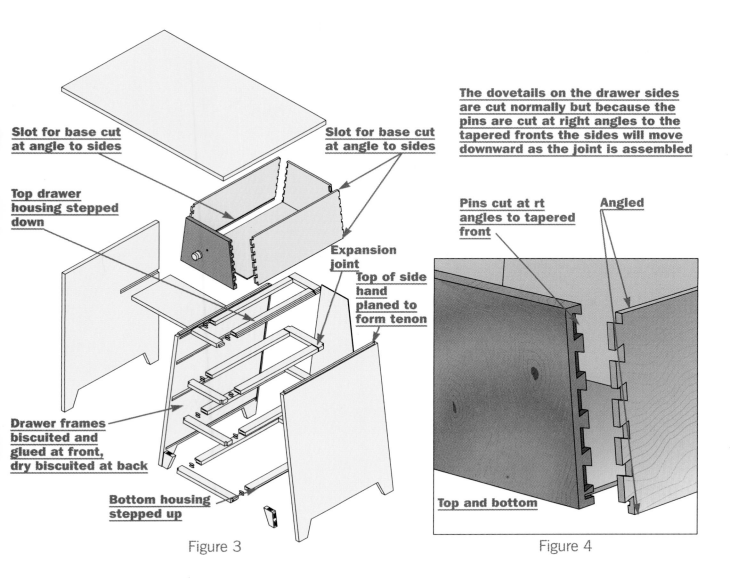

Slot for base cut at angle to sides

Slot for base cut at angle to sides

Top drawer housing stepped down

The dovetails on the drawer sides are cut normally but because the pins are cut at right angles to the tapered fronts the sides will move downward as the joint is assembled

Pins cut at rt angles to tapered front

Angled

Expansion joint

Top of side hand planed to form tenon

Drawer frames biscuited and glued at front, dry biscuited at back

Bottom housing stepped up

Top and bottom

Figure 3

Figure 4

getting it together

accurately using the full size drawing on hardboard, finished and check fitted.

Assembly had to be approached with even more care than usual. The top could not be fitted after the frames, because of the angled housings, so the first stage of the gluing up would be the sides, frames, and top, all in one go. I prepared everything, carefully finishing all the pieces I could, and dry fitted the whole thing. I used battens with shallow notches cut into them to hold the sash clamps level and to stop them from slipping.

Cascamite was made up and applied to the front and back of the frame housings (**Fig 3**), leaving the sides of the frames a dry running fit to allow for future movement. As the grain of the top and sides was running in the same direction, glue was applied all along the housings and to the top of the front and back rails of the top frame.

The back was dry fitted to help keep the taper even. The frames and top were positioned and the sash clamps were placed across the front and back. The eveness of the taper was checked by measuring the diagonals, which should be equal,

as with a square construction. A further check was done with the plastic angle setter on each drawer frame and all seemed to be well. The top was held to the top rail using g-clamps, and left overnight to set.

The next day the back was carefully slid out and glue was applied to the slot and the backs of the back rails. The back was replaced and pinned to the rails, glue was then applied to the foot housings and the feet were fitted.

drawing to a close...

Now that the carcass was complete, I fitted the drawer components. The top and bottom of the sides needed to be cut at an angle, (**Fig 4**) so I set the table saw blade and the planer fence to the correct angle using my trusty angle setter. I also cut the slots for the drawer bases on the table saw while the angle was set. Next, I cut and fitted the drawer fronts, remembering that because of the taper anything taken off the bottom edge would also reduce the width. To reduce the height without altering the width, plane the top edge. I then cut the slots in the fronts to take the drawer bases. Using the fronts as a pattern, I cut the backs which were 5mm (^{3}/$_{16}$in) lower than the

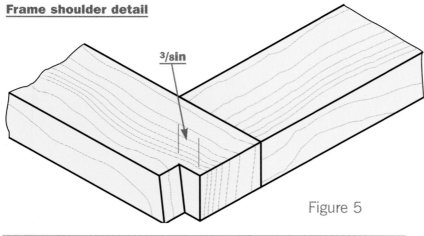

3/8in

Figure 5

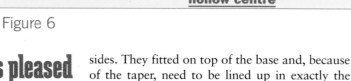

Biscuits

1mm gap at centre

Jointing two pieces showing biscuits and hollow centre

Figure 6

I was pleased with the unusual look of this tapered piece and so was my client

sides. They fitted on top of the base and, because of the taper, need to be lined up in exactly the right place.

I cut strips of 5mm (3/16in) ply 13mm (1/2in) wide, and fitted it in the base slot and cut in the drawer fronts. The backs were cut to the correct height, put on the edge of the bench, and the fronts offered up to them until the backs registered on to the protruding ply. They were then marked with a knife and cut and checked for fit. After the backs had been cut, I oiled the backs of the drawer fronts to help stabilise the burr, applying several coats prior to assembly.

drawer dovetails

The dovetails were marked on the sides, cut just short of the line on the bandsaw, and finished with a chisel. The positioning of the pins was critical as they would be cut at right angles to the tapered front. Consequently the sides would move down the front as the joint was assembled. I marked the horizontal and used a set square to measure the amount of offset.

Allowing for it, I marked the pins on the edges of the drawer fronts. I marked the backs with a set square from the edge of the front, and removed the waste with a router, dovetail saw, and chisel. The joints were glued up and the drawers assembled, with the cedar of Lebanon faced MDF bases glued in all round for extra strength.

Pulls were made from off cuts of burr, and then pegged, glued, and screwed into the fronts. The

drawers and stops were fitted keeping in mind that due to the taper any adjustment to the height from the bases would result in a corresponding reduction in the width of the drawer.

fuming to the finish

The carcass was wiped over with white spirit to remove any glue marks and left to dry before being hand sanded to 320 grit. All surplus glue was removed and the piece double-checked for marks, blemishes and raised grain. It was then placed in a polythene tent, with about 5fl oz of 890 ammonia in saucers, and left for 24 hours. This process must be undertaken with care and eye protection should always be worn as ammonia has a particularly adverse effect on the eyes and contact causes permanent damage.

To finish, I used Danish oil as it brings out the deep richness of the figure and colour of the burr while also giving a silky finish to the mahogany. The burr was quite porous and the oil penetrated well in to the wood, helping to stabilise it. The first coat was liberally applied and refreshed every 15 to 20 minutes until no more would soak in. The burr took considerably more oil and coats than the less porous mahogany. The chest was wiped off with a soft cloth between coats to prevent oil building up on the surface and then left to harden for 24 hours in a warm, dry place. To finish, the surface was cut back with a Scotchbrite grey pad, further light coats applied every 24 hours and then cut back again until the desired effect was achieved.

Designer drawers

MAKER

Roger Smith

Roger Smith uses his router to make a chest of drawers

I WAS looking for a project where I could use a number of stored macracapa boards, and I got my chance when I was asked to make a chest of drawers to complement a piece made many years earlier by the renowned Alan Peters. Believe it or not, that piece was in macracapa.

Sawing

I acquired the six foot log of macracapa in the early 90s, and had it sawn into 2in planks. Now I needed boards ranging from 10mm to 22mm. This meant re-sawing the boards.

Deeping a thick board to give two thin ones is rarely a good idea, but as the timber had not been kiln-dried I was happy to take the risk.

I used a bandsaw at a local sawmill, and was relieved to end up with boards that showed little or no signs of bowing or cupping.

Kilning down to 10% moisture content followed, but if this facility is unavailable, leave the boards in a warm room to acclimatise.

Surface and thickness all carcass, drawer front and drawer side pieces prior to selecting

Unfortunately, macracapa doesn't plane well, so I edge-jointed the boards, and found a cabinet-maker willing to let me pass all the components through his speed sander – a truly excellent machine, but difficult to justify owning one when I can hire someone else's!

I have always admired Alan Peters' work, and I wanted to adopt his method of using through-dovetails for the entire piece, including the drawer fronts and carcass.

What I didn't want to do was cut them by hand. The Leigh Dovetail Jig was about to come to my rescue.

> ## "These dimensions produce a small but perfectly proportioned chest"

◀ *A beautiful chest of drawers with dovetail joints*

▲ *Set the carcass timber up in the jig, note the setting up piece, then ...*

▶ *... carefully rout the pins and tails*

Using the jig

Timber preparation is the key to producing accurate joints, and this rule also applies when using the Leigh Jig. Stock must be of regular thickness, and the ends must be square.

I needed to grade the sizes of the drawer fronts, as I wanted all the joints the same size. When the guide fingers of the jig are at their closest interval, the gauge of the joint is 1in.

Allowing the half-pin either side, this gives drawers of 5¼in, 6¼in, 7¼in and 8¼in. Why not metric you say? Because the Leigh Jig is Canadian, and they still work in inches.

This drawer configuration enabled me to keep an overall height of 34in, a depth of 17in and a width of 21½in. These dimensions produce what I consider to be a small but well proportioned chest.

I was keen to test my new T5 Trend router on the drawers, but needed a more powerful tool for the carcass.

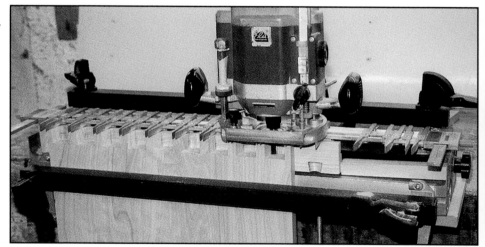

▼ *The housings for the cabinet's backs are routed next*

Tooling up

■ **Leigh Dovetail Jig**
■ **T5 Trend router**
■ **Elu 177 router**
■ **Leigh 100 dovetail cutter**
■ **150 straight bit**
■ **Leigh 80-8 cutter**
■ **2.5mm radius cutter**
■ **A lot of sash cramps**

I resorted to the tried and tested Elu 177, at 1600W a tool that is rather heavy to hold. I needed its ½in collet to hold the Leigh 100 dovetail cutter and corresponding 150 straight bit.

The cutters gave me nine tails over the 17in deep carcass, producing an imposing joint suitable for 22mm thick material.

To avoid tear-out when routing, a long strip of packing is wedged behind the joints to be cut. This keeps all edges crisp, so near perfect joints should follow.

Drawer divisions

I pondered on which method to adopt for the drawer divisions, and plumped for the solid wood housed into the sides.

If I was using an expensive timber I might have thought differently, but solid divisions overcome any of the problems associated with shrinkage.

The shelves stop short of the back when grooving the sides and top, so a 10mm-thick back could be slid in from the bottom at a later date.

I used a stopped housing rather than a 'Leigh'-cut dovetail housing, as I didn't want the joint visible from either the front or back.

To cut the 8mm deep housing I used the Trend router with the straight 8mm shank, ½in diameter cutter.

This is a much nicer tool to use than my large Elu, which doesn't have the soft start of the Trend. In fact, the soft start if so soft and slow that you wonder whether the tool is going to start at all!

"If the shelves are tight in their housing, assembly will become a nightmare"

Cut the housings using a simple jig or fence, cramped as required. The dovetails should be a good fit, but if the shelves are tight in their housing, assembly will become a nightmare.

If you add glue to a tight housing, the joint will often refuse to budge after only few minutes. To help alignment I cut MDF boards to rest on the shelves. This is not essential, but gives an immediate indication that each shelf is fully home in its housing.

The cramping battens positioned opposite each shelf are curved, sometimes called banana bars, so cramping pressure is applied to the middle first. Even so, if the joints are too tight the sides won't pull down in the middle.

This often nerve-wracking part of gluing up is best tackled with a helper, and I found this job was no exception. I used 10 sash cramps, but you should be able to manage with six by moving them around.

It goes without saying that if the carcass is not glued together as it should be, fitting the drawers to run well can be difficult.

Design defence

A piece of furniture with so few decorative mouldings sounds very dull, but with careful timber selection, clean lines and crisp joints, does this piece need any further embellishment?

The end-grain on the drawer fronts is a prominent feature, and would be even more striking if a different-coloured timber had been used for the drawer sides.

Straight-grained mahogany or oak would certainly have made the drawer easier to fit, but the effect could look rather busy.

Perhaps even the teak knobs should have been macracapa, but they lift the piece and give an obvious focal point.

Would I have attempted this project without the aid of a router and a Leigh Jig? Probably not. The added bonus is, unless you are really on the ball, nothing gives it away as machine cut.

Only the drawer backs are not truly correct, but even this could be put down to lack of constructional knowledge, rather than the jig!

▲ *When all the joints are cut the carcass can be glued and cramped, an assistant and a lot of cramps are required*

▲ *Drawer timber is placed in the jig ...*

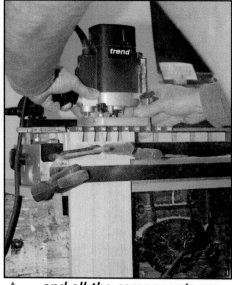

▲ *... and all the components are dovetailed*

Drawer dovetails

Plane the drawer stock to width. Because I had speed sanded it to 13mm thick, the drawer fronts were limited to a maximum of 19mm, as this was the thickest wood the Leigh 80-8 cutter would cut through.

To give drawers an authentic look, the backs need to be narrower than the sides. To achieve this, cut the joints on the backs, but omit the top and bottom half-pin sockets from the sides.

The back can be reduced in width so that the drawer slips can be applied and the bottom slid in. Before assembling, groove the drawer front to take the bottom.

Cutting the back to size before jointing creates problems when aligning pieces in the dovetail jig. So, despite being wasteful, start with all pieces the same width.

I used the Trend router to cut the drawer dovetails, producing excellent fitting joints with no tearing, providing waste wood was cramped either side of the joint being cut.

The grain direction on the waste runs the same way as the drawer component being routed. I found this essential for smooth, vibration-free routing.

"Drawer slips increase the strength and look good"

Drawer slips

It is often said that you should never use cramps when gluing-up drawers. I usually ignore this rule, but you must apply the minimum pressure needed with, preferably, lightweight cramps.

This will avoid distorting the drawer and allow it to be held square while the glue dries.

Drawer slips can be fiddly to make, and may be seen as unnecessary, but I have never been a fan of grooving directly into the drawer sides.

I think drawer slips also increase the strength and look good. More importantly, especially with softwood, they reduce wear by increasing the surface area bearing on the drawer divisions.

When cutting, it is much easier to rout the edge of a wide board and then saw off. This is easier to hold than a thin flexible strip.

Fitting drawers

To fit the drawers, plane the sides with the drawers held as shown. A straight-grain timber would have made life much easier, as tearing meant a lot of sanding was needed.

I sanded the drawer sides quickly with a pad sander, taking care not to round the edges. In general, avoid excessive sanding on drawers. Careful timber selection means sanding can virtually be eliminated altogether.

Remember that good drawer fit is largely determined by how the sides run against the carcass, and not against the drawer divisions. Frequent testing is essential for a good fit.

Trial and error with the drawer positioning revealed that the best effect was achieved by cutting the drawer front into the carcass by 2.3mm. All visible edges of the carcass were rounded over with a 2.5 radius cutter.

▼ **The drawers are cramped together, use cramps that hold rather than pull to avoid distortion**

▼ **Slips for the drawer bottoms are routed then fixed into the drawer boxes**

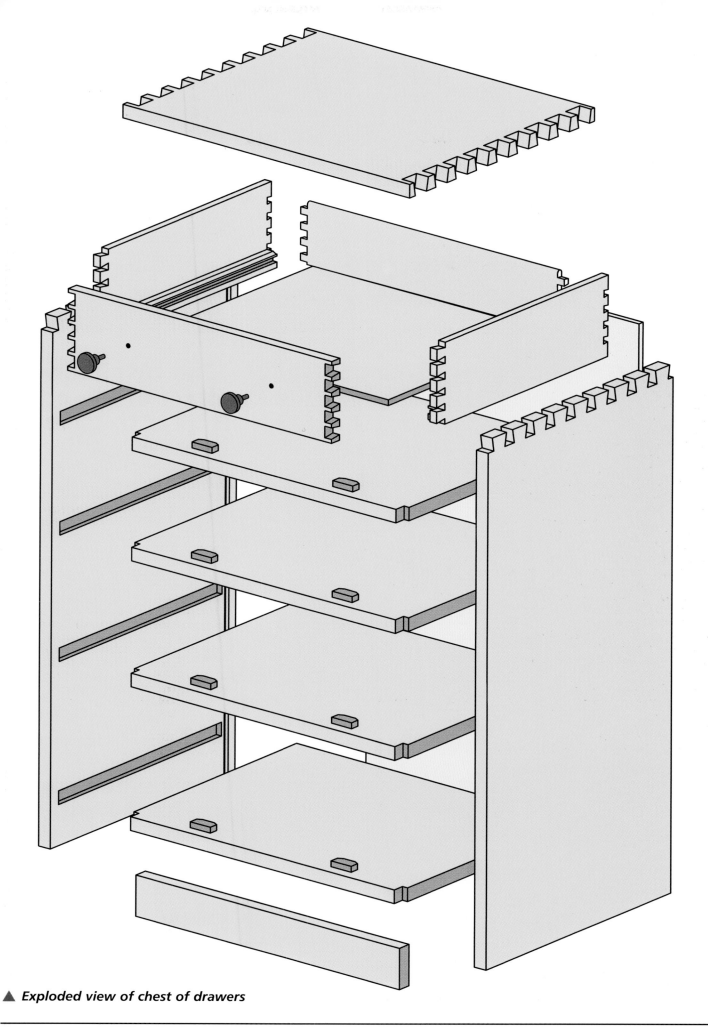

▲ *Exploded view of chest of drawers*

▲ The trusty hand plane is the best tool to use when making the fine adjustments required for drawer fitting

▲ Detail of the drawer back

"The cushioning effect of the air is an attractive feature"

Air flow

As I mentioned earlier, the cabinet back is slid in from the bottom. I glued three of the less attractive boards together to make the back, and held it with three screws passing into the bottom shelf.

Unlike the bottom shelf, the middle shelves are not run right up to the back. This allows air to pass freely up and down the cabinet.

However, when one drawer closes, compressed air tends to push another drawer out. This can be overcome by drilling a hole in the back, but I find the cushioning effect of the air an attractive feature, and customers tend to regard it as a sign of good craftsmanship!

If you don't like one drawer coming out as you push another one in, isolate each drawer by taking the drawer divisions right to the back.

"Only when you are happy with the finish should the final assembly take place"

Finishing touches

The plinth is the simplest part of the project – a short length of wood slotted into shallow gróoves routed into the sides. Remember to rout these two slots, and the three for the back, before assembling the carcass.

A dovetail extravaganza, see bow the graduated drawer sizes enhance the design of the chest

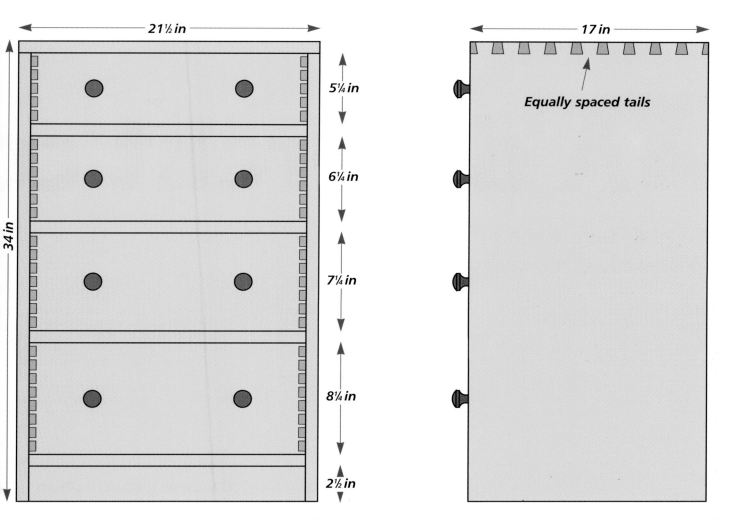

21½ in	17 in
5¼ in	
6¼ in	Equally spaced tails
7¼ in	
8¼ in	
2½ in	
34 in	

▲ **Dimensions of chest**

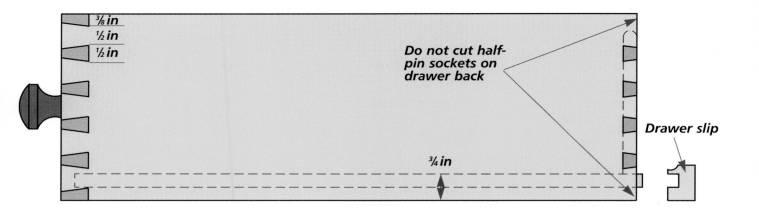

⅜ in
½ in
½ in

Do not cut half-pin sockets on drawer back

Drawer slip

¾ in

▲ **Side elevation of drawer**

Having stuck with the same wood throughout, I decided teak knobs would suit the piece. Simple, 45mm-diameter knobs fixed with a 15mm spigot completed the construction of the chest

It is easier to apply the finish before gluing and screwing the knobs in place.

To retain the light colour of the wood, I chose to spray melamine lacquer.

Danish oil would have been an acceptable alternative, but would have darkened the timber slightly. Whatever finish is chosen, it is easier to apply it with the drawer bottoms, cabinet back

and knobs removed.

The drawer sides and interiors need only a couple of light coats, whereas the top and sides of the cabinet will obviously need a heavier covering.

Only when you are happy with the finish should the final assembly take place.

A different co

Kevin Ley utilises limited space effectively with a tiger-oak corner cupboard

EVEN though we had a good clear-out when we moved from our Yorkshire house to a smaller cottage in Shropshire, display space for my wife's china collection was at a premium. However, we decided that a corner of the new cottage's sitting room was ideally suited for a hanging display cupboard.

Generally corner cupboards don't really provide as much space as initially appears because the shape of the shelves restricts the display and storage possibilities. It would not be a problem in our case though, as the china items were well suited to a small display area.

Design
As the cupboard was to display specific items we spent some time arranging each shelf's contents on an area marked out to represent the shelf size and shape, changing the area and the display until we arrived at the optimum sizes and spacings. I use the same method when making bookcases – avoiding making adjustable shelves, which are rarely moved after initially being filled, and which weaken the structure. Far better to line up all the items which are to go in it, and work out the shelf spacings beforehand, allowing much stronger, permanent, shelf fixing.

In this case, once we had worked out the number and sizes of the shelves, we measured the spacing required between them. The fronts of the cupboard were made quite narrow to give as large an opening as possible for the shelves. This resulted in a tall and slim design, making an elegant overall display, which fitted well into its corner of the room.

Timber
I had been making some cottage doors (which will be covered in a future article) out of brown oak. While sorting through it to find evenly matched colour for the doors I came across some pieces of 'Stripey' or 'Tiger' oak.

Brown oak is normal English oak that has been attacked by the Beef Steak fungus (*Fistulian hepatica*). The fungus enters via an open wound or damaged area. Despite feeding off the tree it does little real damage, instead taking sustenance from the sap and

excreting waste chemicals into the wood to cause an attractive colour change to a rich, dark, golden brown. Incidentally, though not poisonous, the fungus tastes revolting – not at all like steak!

Tiger or Stripey oak is again normal English oak, which has been attacked by the same fungus, but the colour change has not taken place evenly, resulting in tiger-like stripes and streaks. The stripey effect is not even, and requires careful selection to obtain a pleasing effect. Both woods are relatively rare and very attractive.

After a lot of careful selection and marking out, there was just sufficient tiger oak to give a nice even effect to the most visible surfaces of the cupboard.

Marking out from template

Preparation
First I drew the outline of the top and base to real size on hardboard. The sides and fronts were housed directly into the top and base allowing a 13mm (½in) overhang; the sides fitted into the fronts in 6mm x 15mm (¼in x ⅝in) housings, while the left and right-hand sides fitted together at the back in another 6mm x 15mm (¼in x ⅝in) housing. The shelves were also let into the sides and fronts in 6mm x 15mm (¼in x ⅝in) housings. Drawing this all to size on the hardboard allowed accurate measurements to be taken for all the component parts. I then cut a template for the top, base and shelves to make marking and cutting out easier. Next, all the carcass timber was faced and thicknessed to 15mm (⅝in), and where necessary jointed to width.

Biscuits were used to strengthen the joins

and prevent any slippage when clamping up. I used a biscuit cutter on my small Trend router to cut the slots for the biscuits. The hardboard templates were used to mark out the triangular pieces most economically. The grain direction of the shelves, top and base should be parallel to the line of the front [see diagram] to allow for movement across the grain when jointed into the sides.

I chose the best faces of the sides, top, and base for the inside of the cupboard, as the other faces would not be seen in normal use.

Carcass construction
The sides and shelves were cut to size, the front edges of the shelves were rounded over and the shoulder cut in where they fit into the fronts (note the way that this shoulder is cut in – see diagram). The inside edges of the fronts were finished square, and the tops shouldered.

The 15mm x 6mm (⅝in x ¼in) housings were cut in the fronts to take the sides, and in the right hand side at the back, to take

Rounding edges on a router table

ner

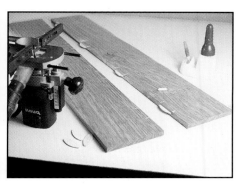

Jointing side pieces with biscuits

the left side. Then the 15mm x 6mm (⅝in x ¼in) housings were cut in both sides and the fronts to take the shelves. All these pieces were sanded to a finish at this point, before assembly.

Next the top and base were cut to size and shape, and the housings for the fronts and sides cut 13mm (½in) in from the edge. The front edges were rounded over, and both pieces finished.

Assembly

The entire cabinet was now dry assembled to check the fit of all joints and any necessary adjustments made. Assembly was in two stages; first PVA glue was applied to the housings in the fronts and sides, and the fronts, sides, and shelves fitted together. To help keep the whole thing true I dry fitted the top and base. Clamps were applied from front to back, everything was checked for trueness and left to set.

After the glue had set I applied PVA to the top and base housings, fitted them to the sides and fronts, and clamped from top to base. Again I checked all was square and left it to set.

Decorative strip

I decided to add a small decorative strip to the top of the cupboard, and in order to support it, needed to add a crosspiece under the front of the top. This was cut to size, with a 45° butt joint at each end to fit to the inner edges of the fronts, and glued and clamped to the top.

A saw cut 3mm (⅛in) deep was cut every 19mm (¾in) in a strip of oak 19mm x 6mm (¾in x ¼in) to leave a series of small raised pieces, which form the decorative strip. I marked the first cut, and using a register pencil mark on the fence of the radial arm

All hung up and nowhere to go

saw, made the remaining cuts. A similar result could be achieved, albeit more slowly, by marking each cut and making the cut by hand using a tenon saw with a wide set and a depth stop clamped to the blade. Alternatively a jig could be made and the cuts made with a router fitted with a 3mm (⅛in) straight cutter.

The strip was sanded and finished and the centre piece cut to size, with a 22½° butt join face at each end, and glued to the cross strip. The two sidepieces were then cut, fitted, and glued to the fronts of the cup-

Close-up of decorative strip

board. The join between the sides and the front of the strip should be in the same position on the raised decorative square on each side or it will look unbalanced.

Finish

I have always liked the look of old, oiled oak and when I tried boiled linseed oil on some scraps of this brown oak it looked fantastic. I hand sanded the whole cupboard, checking carefully for glue ooze and marks, particularly on the visible inside faces. I then sanded down to 240 grit, wiped it all over with white spirit, and checked again. Once satisfied that the finish was good I applied a liberal coat of warm, boiled linseed oil. Warming the oil reduces viscosity and helps penetration.

The old oiling adage of 'Once an hour for a day, once a day for a week, once a week for a month and once a year thereafter' is not far out. The first coat was liberally applied, left to soak in, and refreshed every 15 to 20 minutes until it would take no more (4 - 6 coats). It was then wiped off with a soft cloth. No oil must be allowed to build up

Cutting decorative strip on radial arm saw

on the surface, and the piece was then left to harden in a dry, warm place for 24 hours.

The surface was cut back with a Scotchbrite grey pad and further light coats applied every 24 hours. This too was cut back with the Scotchbrite pad, making sure that there was no build up of oil on the surface. Once the desired effect was achieved I gave it a final coat of Danish oil to speed up the hardening process.

After a few days this last coat was cut back and buffed with a soft cloth to a nice soft sheen. Future care would be an annual light coat of teak oil.

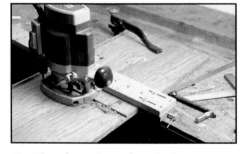

Cutting housings for shelves

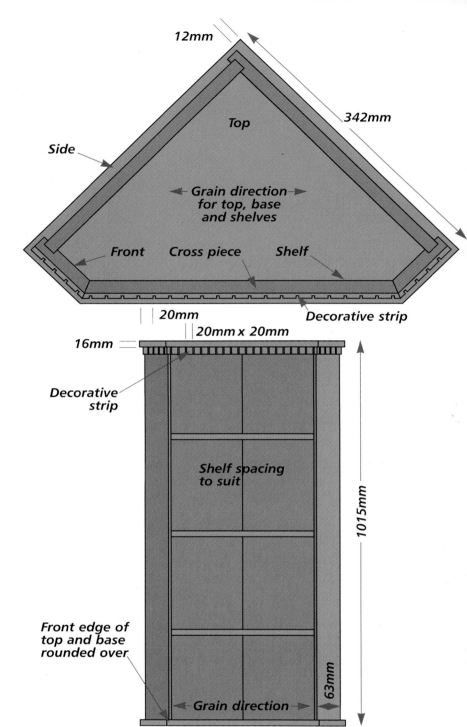

The finished article

To hang the cupboard I drilled counter sunk holes through the sides just behind the fronts at the base, and in the top back corner. These are all places where the screw heads would not be seen. These holes were marked through to the wall, which was drilled and plugged. It was then screwed through the sides, into the wall plugs, to hang firmly in position.

My wife was duly called for the seal of approval, and she completed the project by putting the china in place. Mind you, I think I prefer it empty – to show off that lovely wood!

The man himself by the finished article

Dressing it up

Phillip Gullam puts together a medium-sized brown oak display cabinet for the kitchen

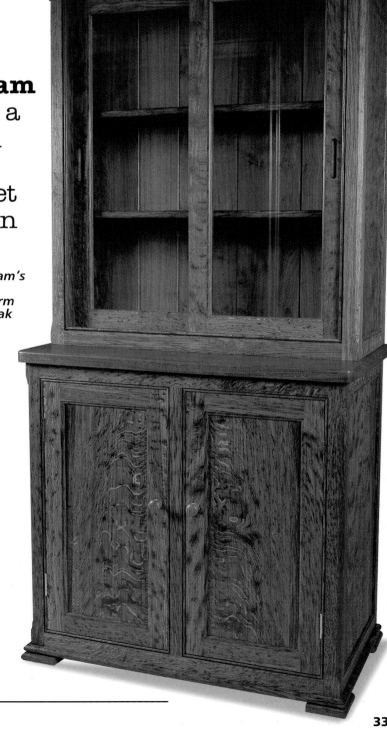

Phillip Gullam's dresser has instant charm in brown oak

A FRIEND of mine was getting married, so I decided to make a kitchen display cabinet as a wedding gift. The kitchen was small, so I designed a piece that wasn't too large and overbearing for the confined area, but at the same time was not so small as to be insignificant.

Design

I wanted to recreate a traditional cabinet, which would fit well within their 150-year-old ex-miner's cottage. I decided to use oak, and made several unsuccessful trips to the timber yard before I found some excellent planks of brown oak lurking under a stack of uninspiring timber.

The cabinet carcasses are made up of six frames. The joints are traditional mortice and tenon, with a simple bead on the inside edge.

Cutting

Carefully select the timber, as you want to choose the right figure and colour for the areas of the cabinet most on show. Some of the pieces are changed around once machined, so it is advisable to have a few good planks spare – they also prove useful for setting up on.

It is a good idea to plan out the whole job in advance, as there are quite a few

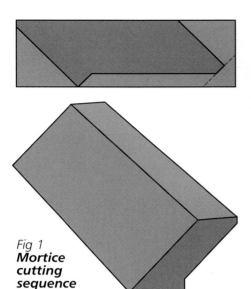

Fig 1
Mortice cutting sequence

Note beading on rails

Close-up of the bottom door

different stages which need to be completed before gluing-up.

When marking out the cutting list, note where the front and side frames join. They need to look like a piece of 50 by 50, so try to arrange the grain so that the joint doesn't stick out like a sore thumb. The bases, top and panels are quite wide and need jointing. They should be glued at the very start of the job so that they are ready when needed.

Once the timber is machined and marked out clearly, mark out and cut the mortices and tenons. When cutting the joint, remember that 8mm for the bead will be cut off the mortices.

Once the mortice and tenons have been cut, a 3.2mm radius bead is cut on the inside edges, except for the top front frame. This has a separate bead that is put on later. The best way to avoid damaging breakout when routing the bead is to set the cutter through a fence.

Mitres

Next, cut the mitres. These should be done with care, otherwise the finished frame will have tight joints but open mitres. I cut my beads on a guillotine, but they can be done equally as well with a mitre template.

Run an 8mm groove through the inside edge of the side frames for the panels. This is done on the cross rails to form the shoulder, but should be stopped on the stiles. Once again, setting the cutter through a fence will avoid breakout.

Where the side frames join onto the front frame, the stiles are biscuited and glued. Gluing them together at this stage of construction means you can get even pressure along the whole joint.

Panels

Next come the panels. They are just plain panels with a rebate to make them flush on the back of the frame. They should be

machined oversize at the start of the job, and made to their final dimension thickness once the groove has been cut in the rails.

The depth of the cut is 1 to 1.5mm more than the groove. The panels need to be 2mm less on the height, and 3mm less on the width. Set up the rebate cutter on one of the panels before cutting it to size.

Sand the panels before cutting the rebate as sanding afterwards can cause a sloppy fit. To stop the corners looking too heavy, machine a 20mm bevel, then carve a small scallop to neatly finish the ends. The scallop begins in line with the bead

and is 25mm long. Then cut the depth of the bevel to stop any breakout when routing.

Once the bevel has been cut, use a ½in chisel to scallop down to the width of the bevel, but 3mm above it. The step should then be rounded-over using a sharp chisel.

The bottom doors are hinged with brass butt hinges which you can rebate out before gluing-up. I used a jig for this.

Cut a rebate in the back of the side frame stiles for the tongue and groove back. This is made about 1.5mm deeper than the tongue groove and half the thickness of the frame.

"The front of the shelf and frame also need to be biscuit jointed"

Handles and meeting stile detail

Note fielding on door panel

Before gluing-up I find it easier to joint the frames for the top and bottom shelves – I use biscuits for jointing.

I find it easier to get in with a biscuit jointer and cut the grooves at this stage, before the panels are in. The beads and edges are then sanded, and the side frames glued. Once these are set, clean the insides.

Base

Glue-up the front frame next. Doing it this way avoids the large frames having to be clamped on their sides. Cut the top and bottom shelves to length, and machine a groove both ends, so as to slide the shelf in on the biscuits. The front of the shelf and the frame also need to be biscuited. The base width is less the thickness of the rebate for the back.

Next, glue the base to the frames, cleaning off any excess glue. You now have the base to the dresser, but it will still be unstable at the top of the back. A rail needs to be put in to make the whole structure rigid. For this, use a piece of 70 by 22mm oak with a 60mm wide dovetail, 15mm long. The rail is also used for fixing the tongue and groove back.

"The joints are traditional mortice and tenon with a simple bead on the inside edge"

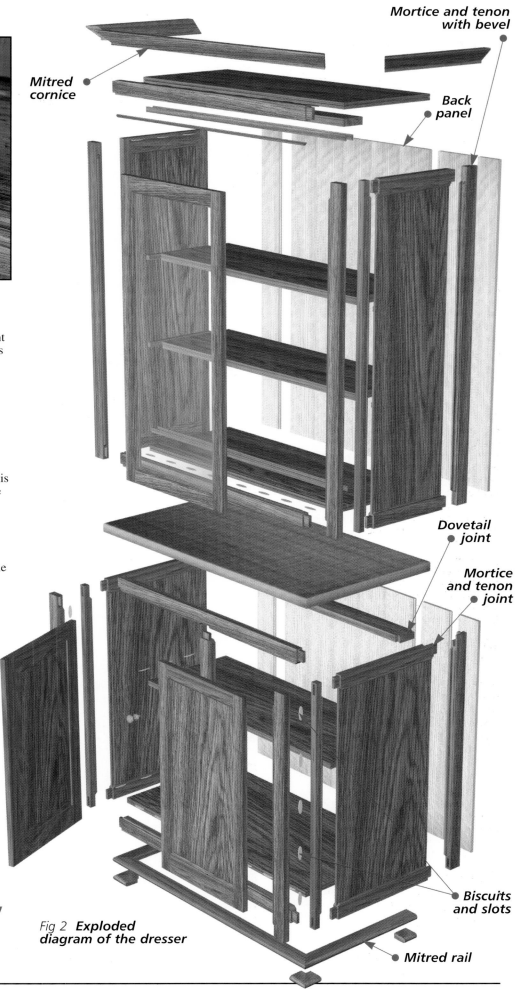

Mortice and tenon with bevel

Mitred cornice

Back panel

Dovetail joint

Mortice and tenon joint

Biscuits and slots

Fig 2 **Exploded diagram of the dresser**

Mitred rail

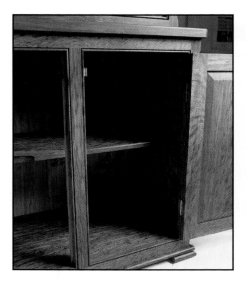

Glass sliding doors save space in a small kitchen

Cornice, scallop and bevel detail make the piece a little special

small space I wanted to keep the actual display area as prominant as possible, hence the sliding doors.

As they overlap, you only lose the width of a stile instead of two – not much, but enough to make a difference. The sliding doors also save having large glazed doors swinging out into a narrow kitchen.

With the doors glued-up, the base doors are fitted with a small gap around them of 1.5mm overall height and a fag-paper on the width. The top doors should be made 4mm shorter over the height, to allow for the rollers which they slide on.

It is important to get the width right for the sliding doors. Make up a full-size rod to ensure the sizes are correct. The right-hand door overlaps the left one by 50mm, so all that can be seen of the right-hand stile of the left door is the moulding.

Feet

To stop the base looking too heavy, make small double bull nose feet. The first bull nose should go around the whole cabinet, and be 15mm bigger than the cabinet. The corners are mitred, then glued. The second bull nose comprises two corners and the back feet. The corners are two pieces, 70mm long, mitred together. Once the mitres are set, a 9mm roundover should be machined top and bottom. I find it best to do this on a router table and a fence. The pieces are then sanded and screwed in place.

Top

The top of the dresser is slightly different as it also has a top shelf – the same construction processes should be used for fixing these. The top shelf is flush with the top of the frame and the bottom shelf flush with the top of the bottom rail, as this is what the doors will slide onto.

Before gluing the shelves in, 3mm grooves need to be cut for the sliding doors. The bottom shelf has a groove cut in it for plates to sit within, then the top and bottom shelves are glued in.

Sliding doors

The dresser carcasses are nearly complete. The doors are scribed mortice and tenon. Cut the tenons and scribe on a tenoner.

Machine the stile profiles and cut the mortices. The panels for the base doors are plain on the face and raised on the back. As the dresser is made to fit in a

Fitting doors

Rebate the doors after they have been glued-up for the glass, using a flush trim cutter with a bottom bearing following the groove made with the stile moulding. They are then given small rollers to help them slide more easily. Before they are fitted, the guides need to be made out of 3mm oak. The door should run smoothly along the guides – so make sure the fit is not too tight.

They are then fitted – held in place by beading which is fixed separately onto the frame. The upright piece is wider as the left door goes behind it. Once everything is fitted and finished, fix it in place permanently, except for the top piece, which is screwed in place so that, if necessary, the doors can be removed.

Once the doors are in place, mark the heights of the shelves. They are set so the distance between the shelves is equal when you look through the glass, but not when you open the door. The pulls in the doors are made using the same cutter as the plate grooves for the shelves.

The sliding door pull

Tongue and groove boarding in the back, from the inside

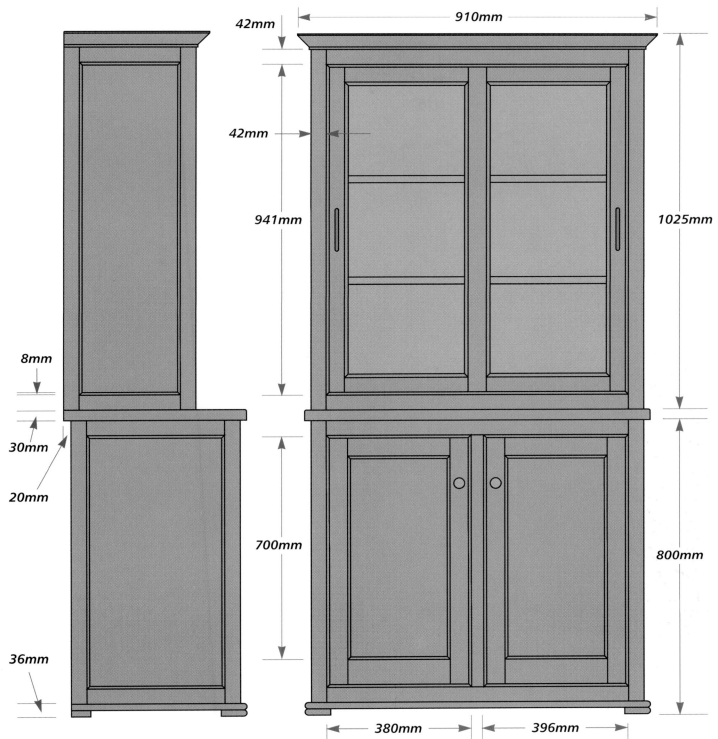

Worktop

The shelves rest on the battens which are screwed and plugged to the side frames. It may sound obvious, but the shelf width has to be set just behind the innermost door.

The top of the dresser sits on an Iroko (Milicia excelsa) worktop. It doesn't give you much working area but becomes a handy place to put mugs and glasses, ensuring nobody can open the doors and break a favourite.

The top is fixed down with shrinkage plates through the frame at the front. The backs are made up from 13mm thick oak tongue and groove boards, fixed in to allow for movement.

My friends were over the moon with the cabinet, and I must admit, I was quite smug – no wedding list to ponder over and a chance to use one of my favourite timbers.

Fig 3 **Front and side view of the dresser**

Finishing

The cornice is made up out of 25mm timber. Before the feet are glazed and magnetic catches are fixed, the whole dresser has three coats of 50.50 linseed oil and white spirit.

The shelves have two coats of Danish oil to seal them – this stops boxes of cereal soaking up the linseed oil. The oil takes a couple of weeks to dry completely, then the doors are glazed using 4.4 toughened glass. Finally, the doors are hung and knobs and catches are fitted.

Clients ask for the oddest things

A novel solution

TUTOR

Mark Constanduros

Mark Constanduros builds a corner bookcase

Cutting the curve as close to the line as possible

Bookcases are always a popular piece of furniture, especially amongst avid readers. This particular piece has been made to fill a gap that was virtually useless for anything else and also to be as versatile as possible to accommodate a variety of irregular book sizes.

This is a very simple piece and has the benefit of requiring a jig to be made which, if looked after, will be able to be used time and time again. As you can see, the bottom of the bookcase has a curve going in towards the wall to reduce the appearance of heaviness and to remove the sharp edge that would have been left. It also creates a bit of interest.

Jiggery-pokery

To create the curve you can either sketch it out on a board or use a piece of graph paper. For this particular bookcase the curves were different because of the position in the client's house. It would be better if both curves on the bookcases were the same. When you have decided on your curve, transfer it to a sheet of MDF which you have made wider than required so the bearing can run off. Try and cut as close to the line as possible and then using a sanding disc on a pillar drill carefully clean up the edge to pro-

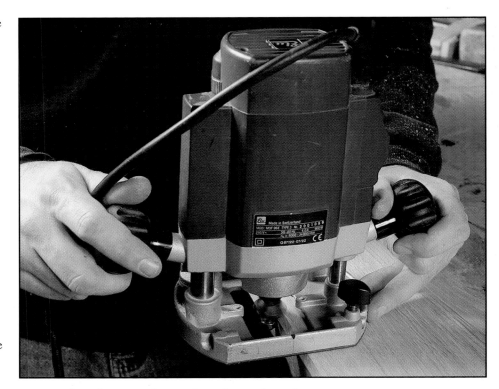

An overhead router is used to clean the edge

There can never be...   **...enough attention to detail**

Cutting rebates in the bookcase sides to hold the shelves

"...fill with quality novels and a dash of pulp fiction."

vide a smooth and even curve to run the bearing off. You can also clean the curve up by modifying your sanding block so that it is curved to suit the jig. On the same jig, mark out where the housing joints will be so that the sides can be screwed to the jigs without leaving any holes on the finished article. Remember to make left and right-handed sides by using both sides of the jig.

Cutting sides

Now that the jig's built and the timber's cut and machined to the cutting list, the sides can be laid on and the curve marked at the base of the side. Cut the curve out as close to the line as possible and then screw the side down on the jig where the holes have been placed to coincide with the housings. I used an overhead router but you can always use a bearing-guided trimmer to clean the edge. This saves on sanding. Now do the same to the other side, creating a left and a right for both bookcases.

Housing joints

To cut out the housing joints you will need a router, an 8mm collet and an 18mm cutter with an 8mm shank. Having a larger shank will lessen the vibration of the cutter when cutting the joints. By now you will have realised that you are cutting a 25mm (1in) housing with an 18mm cutter. A strip of wood 7mm thick and long enough to act as a second fence is also required. A large cutter is not always ideal in a small hand-held router, so here's a small tip that can aid in some "tweaking" during the job: for the first bookcase the top shelf is 200mm (8in) high, the middle shelf is 250mm (10in) high and the bottom shelf is 300mm (12in) high. For the smaller bookcase the top shelf is 200mm (8in) high and the bottom shelf is 350mm (14in) high. Using a strip of MDF as your router guide, position and cramp the required distance from the edge of the router base to the tip of the cutter. This should position the cutter ready to cut the housing. Remember to stop the housing 20mm short of the front edge, and then you can start the procedure. After cutting the first groove to a depth of 12mm, place the strip of wood machined to 7mm against the face of the MDF guide. This will push the router over to create the 25mm (1in) housing. When one is done repeat the operation for all the other housings except the top joint, which will be fixed using No20 biscuits and a series of screws.

The shelves

Next cut out a 15mm nick on the front edge of the shelves. This will act as a stop and leave the edge of the shelves 5mm back from the front edge of the sides. This creates a break in the look of the piece and

Cornicing cut on a spindle moulder

should be 10mm (3/8in) deep to allow for the thickness of the back boards and 18mm wide to allow for a screw to fix the back boards in place. With the rebate done you can now trim the shelves to width so they finish at the back of the housing.

Putting it all together

You can now dry assemble the bookcase and cramp everything in place. Measure the internal width and cut the top shelf to length and then mark out three biscuit positions and three screw holes. Make sure the screw holes are slightly above centre so that the cornice will cover them later. Keeping the bookcase together, mark out all the stops for the chamfer on the inside face of the sides. This chamfer runs all the way round the outside edge but remember to stop short at the top. Now sand up all the inside faces and mask off the joints ready to stain. It's easier to stain with the components separated. When that's done, glue the bookcases together.

Cornice and Backboards

Next step is to make and cut the cornice. The one I used was created on the spindle moulder, but it's possible to create your own with a series of different cutters. You could even buy a ready-made moulding. Set up the bookcases as they will be hanging on the wall, but separate them by about 15mm. This helps make them look like two separate units. Two battens are needed to run down the inside corner to keep the units apart, but also to hide the wall through the gap.

With the units in position the cornice can be cut. To fit it to the carcass cut some blocks with a 45° angle and glue and screw in place. Make sure the cornice covers the screw holes.

The back boards can now be rebated and overlapped, or tongue and grooved, depending on what you prefer. I use both ideas but on this particular piece it was the simple overlap. To allow for the boards to expand and contract leave a gap of about 2mm and screw the boards in place. With all the components

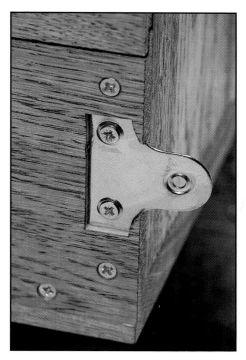

Mirror plates are set in flush

now in place, check that everything fits. Now mark out the positions for the mirror plates which should be placed towards the outermost points and set in so they will sit flush when the bookcase is placed against the wall. To hold the bottom in place mark a couple of holes in the bottom corners where they will be covered by the books, and countersink them. Brass screws would look a little nicer than slotted ones here.

The Finish

The last operation is to dismantle everything and do the final sanding and staining. To finish, use a couple of layers of Danish oil and then a good wax. In this particular case a fine satin lacquer was used.

Now hang the finished piece on the wall and fill with quality novels and a dash of pulp fiction.

Unseen sturdy cornice supports add strenghth

helps in lining up as well as cleaning up. After doing this using the same 18mm cutter, cut out a rebate on the inside edge of the bookcase sides from top to bottom of the bottom shelf housing. This rebate

CUTTING LIST

(all dimensions in mm)

2 sides	950	265	25
3 shelves	744	250	25
1 shelf	720	250	25
5 backboards	850	151	10

(approximately , if you are going to tongue and groove)

2 sides	660	265	25
2 shelves	444	250	25
1 shelf	420	250	25
4 backboards	625	109	10

(approximately , if you are going to tongue and groove)

Approximately 2.5 metres of cornice
4 mirror plates

Fantastic filing

Anthony Bailey

tidies away your paperwork with a compact filing cabinet

MAKER
Anthony Bailey

DO you keep all your vital papers in one of those steel or plastic lock up cases designed for domestic paperwork? Not very big is it? A two-drawer full-size filing cabinet would be ideal, so do as I've done and make a neat compact unit which can fit under a desk or stand by itself.

Measurements

Like any piece of furniture with a spe-cialised containing function, the internal measurements are the critical ones, if you can't fit your suspension files it isn't any use at all!

So, take a standard-width suspension file (there are some sub-size ones designed to save space), the critical dimensions are the 390mm centre-to-cen-tre distance of the cutouts that slide on the rails in the drawer, the height of the file from the bottom to the cutout (237mm), and the height from this point to the top of the ID tab clipped on top (about 22mm). Everything else is deter-mined by these sizes.

A fairly deep unit of 570mm means that with one drawer out it is unlikely to tip over. If this unit is fitted under a desk you can make it shallower to suit. Because it's freestanding there is an overhang with an ovolo moulded edge, for under-desk use the top can be flush.

A wooden filing cabinet fits in well with other furniture for the home office

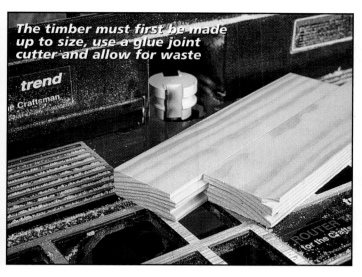

The timber must first be made up to size, use a glue joint cutter and allow for waste

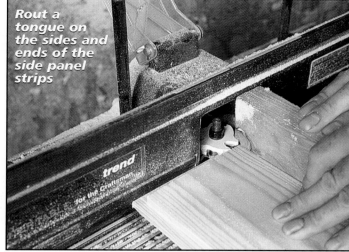

Rout a tongue on the sides and ends of the side panel strips

The overall height of 690mm should just fit under a desk and give enough height for two drawers. If it is a bit tight you could reduce the plinth height of 70mm slightly, or block up the desk.

The width of 500mm is about 19mm wider than that needed to accommodate the files in their drawers, and the 12mm plus 12mm thickness of the runners. Any difference is made up with packers and a bead edge moulding is applied to the inside carcass faces to cover the packers.

All stock is standard 150 by 25mm prepared softwood, which gives a finished thickness of about 20mm. Cut all carcass parts overlength and overwidth.

"A fairly deep unit means that with one drawer out it is unlikely to tip over"

With a slotting cutter, rout the biscuit jointing slots in the edges of the bottom

Tooling up

- Slotting cutter
- Profile and scribe cutters
- Rebate cutter
- Panel raising cutter
- Straight cutter
- Glue joint cutter

Hafele runners and furniture fittings are obtainable in small quantities to order, or ex-stock, from Brighton Tools & Fixings, tel 01273 562020.

As the biscuit slots are set a way in from the edge, matching slots for the bottom must be cut in the sides, using a straight cutter

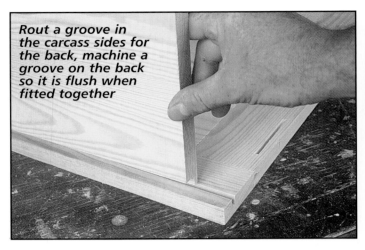

Rout a groove in the carcass sides for the back, machine a groove on the back so it is flush when fitted together

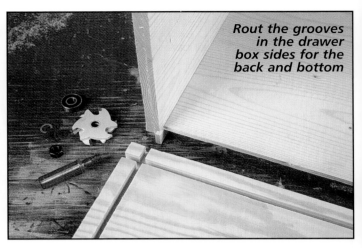

Rout the grooves in the drawer box sides for the back and bottom

Base, panels, sides

Start with the internal base, top and back panels and drawer front panels which are jointed together. You need to allow for the overlap in the joints. Set up a glue joint cutter in the router table, do some test cuts to ensure it is properly centred, then machine all edges to be joined.

Do one edge then flip the board over to do the other edge. Glue, assemble and cramp all pieces. Any misalignment shows and will need thorough belt sanding to level it once dry.

Next tackle the sides. Use a tongue and groove or variable groove set to make the frame, leaving a slot of 6 to 9mm width, and a depth of 10 to 13mm, with tongues on the rail ends to match.

The centre boards are the same thickness and need a bevel machined on all long edges to give a V-groove effect when assembled. First machine all the tongue and grooves, except those around the outside edges.

Instead, assemble all the boards and then cut to the right size before machining a tongue all round the outside. Do this before V-grooving to avoid breakout. Set up a V-point cutter in the table, the bevel should not be too deep or it will affect the tongue and groove.

Rout the V-grooves, including the outer edges, then assemble together and glue the frame around the centre boards. Cramp up, check for square and leave to dry on a flat surface.

Cut all panels to size except the back panel, place together in a lying down attitude, and make some strike marks at 150 to 200mm intervals for biscuit jointing. Use a biscuit cutter with the correct bearing for size '20' biscuits and machine the slots.

Run a groove all around the back of the carcass to tongue the back panel in place. Cut the back panel to the internal size, plus the tongue on all edges.

All internal surfaces should now be thoroughly sanded, not to a fine finish as they will not be very visible. Apply glue to the biscuits but leave the back panel loose to allow for shrinkage. Cramp up the carcass, check for square and make sure it is not 'in wind'.

Wipe off excess glue and leave to dry. The plinth strip is also biscuited to the bottom panel. You now have a box.

Belt sand the exterior surfaces with the grain and orbital sand with a medium grit, leave the fine sanding till later on. To complete the carcass, run a moulding around the top edge (this can be done earlier on using the router table).

"The bevel should not be too deep or it will affect the tongue and groove"

Drawers

Measure the inside of the carcass to check the dimensions will be adequate to hold the two drawers. Two drawer boxes are needed, to which decorative front panels will be fixed. Make the drawer depth less by the thickness of the applied front panel and then another 5mm, so there is no danger of the fronts sticking out proud when installed.

The drawer height will allow both drawers and the overhanging fronts to clear each other when pulled out. The sides are full depth and overlap the front and back to resist the stress of drawer opening.

Use the panel raising cutter to create the drawer fronts

The components of the filing cabinet ready to fit together

Tongue and groove the drawer's sides, fronts and backs and also the bases. Run a groove around all the inside faces. The top of the groove should be 21mm up from the bottom so the bases with their offset tongue will be flush on the underside when fitted.

Dry assemble and measure the size of the bases allowing for the tongues. Cut to size and rout a tongue all round.

Sand internal surfaces to a finish, glue and cramp the drawers together, leaving the base loose, check for square and leave to set. Sand each drawer to a finish on the outside.

I used Tonk strip (library strip) for the files to hang on. To position them, refer to an actual file and mark groove positions on the long top edges of each drawer.

Use a 2mm groover on an arbor with a bearing giving a 9.5mm cut depth in a ¼in router. Sit a drawer on its side, set the cutter depth and carefully run right along the edge. Cut the Tonk strip to length and use small countersunk screws to fit it.

Drawer fronts

The drawer fronts have two raised panels. Cut and plane the frame pieces to width and also to length. The object is to make the

fronts to fit the carcass opening tightly, they will be trimmed for a running fit later.

The rails need to be 19mm overlength as they are scribed into the stiles. Do the scribing cuts first on the router table, ensuring there is a backing piece to prevent breakout. Fit the profile cutter, exchanging cutter and bearing positions if it is a reversible set, or raise the height if you have a combination

set. Do test cuts to get a flush joint and machine one edge of each piece.

Dry fit the frames and measure the panel sizes, which should be 2mm less in each direction for an easy fit, and cut to size. Fit a panel raiser in the table, a through fence will give continuous support for smooth, straight-edged cut.

Machine the panel in several passes so

"If the stiles have been left overlength trim off the horns"

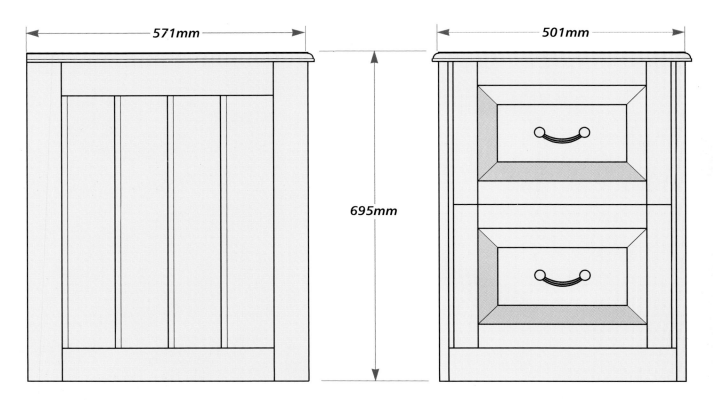

▲ Approximate dimensions of a filing cabinet, adjust to suit

the router isn't overstressed, starting with the crossgrain passes each time so the long passes remove any tearout.

Dry assemble the each panel to check how well they fit together.

Take the front panel apart then sand all the mouldings and the front and back of each panel. Then glue up and reassemble, checking for square. Once the glue is dry the frame's faces can be sanded. If the stiles have been left overlength trim off the 'horns'.

Finally, use some slim packers to position each drawer front in place one above the other, using the saw to trim them until they are a comfortable fit with a 1.5mm to 2mm gap all round.

Runners

Take the filing cabinet runners and fix them inside the carcass with short twinfast screws. Use packing strips, (I found 9.5mm ply was perfect), so that each drawer will be centred in the carcass. The actual height position isn't critical, though midway up each drawer would be about right, although they have to be level and the same height on both sides of course.

▼ Fit on the Tonk strip for the files to suspend from

Make a template on a piece of hardboard the internal height of the carcass with the runner positions and the drawers and the drawer fronts, so you can get the positioning just right to allow the drawers to clear each other.

By opening and closing each runner it is possible to find the fixing holes. The Hafele Accuride runners I used are particularly good in this respect, being very easy to fit. Ensure the screws are the right size and go in square so the heads don't protrude and catch on the moving sections of runner, note that there is a plastic receiver at the back of each runner which holds the drawer closed.

Rest the lower drawer on some blocks at the right height and fix the runners to it flush with the front. Repeat the operation on the upper drawer using higher supports, referring to your template so the positioning is correct.

Fit the handles to the panelled drawer fronts with the bolts or nuts recessed in on the back. Then drill four holes in each drawer-box front at the pilot diameter of the screws that will be used to fix the fronts on, make sure the screws will run through where the fatter raised section of panel will be!

Run the screws in so the sharp tips are just exposed and press each drawer front in place, ensuring they have even gapping all round. The marks left by the screw points can be drilled and the fronts screwed on, any slightly misalignment can be straightened with a tap from a hammer, use a block of softwood to protect the drawer front.

Finishing

You can go for a natural pine finish using varnish flatted between coats, or put a stain on first to give it a bit of colour, maybe to match existing furniture. If you do, make sure the carcass is well sanded with no crossgrain scratches, as the stain will show these up. It is easier to remove the drawer boxes and fronts before applying a finish, in particular you can wipe a band of dye down the inside faces of the carcass so it doesn't look too bare inside.

Push the filing unit into position and add files and paperwork – it won't take long to fill!

▼ The finished filing cabinet ready to fill

Cabinet reshuffle

Bill Cain makes a 1920's style cabinet to fit an old door with a difference

Bill Cain

THIS project started as a simple task, or so I thought at the time. I wanted to make a 1920s style cabinet in oak to blend in with existing furniture while incorporating an original glazed door from that period.

The original cabinet carcass was junked years ago because of woodworm, but the door was fine and had a sentimental value, so I decided to keep it for a rainy day. Normally you would make doors to fit a cabinet but this was going to have to be done the other way round, and it was only as I got into it that the extent of the task dawned on me.

Starting off

I removed the glazing, which was about to fall out anyway, and stripped the original finish. I then realised the door was tapered from top to bottom and had a wind in it; in fact nothing was true or square!

The old glazing had to be retained, and the door was far too 'out' to return to square by planing the edges. I decided to leave the door as it was and cater for the taper and wind when making the new carcass.

How is it when you want a truly square carcass it has the tendency to twist otherwise, but when you have to construct it out of square it becomes a problem? After a bit of head scratching I came up with a solution.

Plan of action

I would make the dovetails between the sides and bottom very slightly loose so I could cant the sides and top in to match the door tapers, then use Cascamite for its strength and gap filling properties. The sides and top would be biscuited jointed and glued using PVA.

◀ *Utilising an old but attractive door makes a splendid new piece of furniture*

Tooling up

- *Slotting cutter*
- *Dovetail cutter*
- *Bearing guided rebate cutter*
- *Wealden T4430 'Tonk strip' cutter*
- *Hinge centring bit*

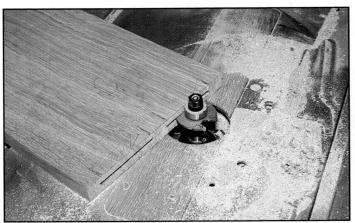

▲ Rout slots for biscuits in the ends of the top

▲ Slot the carcass sides to match, note the angle plate to keep them upright

▲ The dovetail joints on the bottom are left loose so they can be tweaked to fit the door

▲ Library or Tonk strip was chosen for shelf supports seen here with Wealden's proprietary cutter

▲ Rout the slots for the Tonk strip

I could use the door as a jig when gluing up the carcass, and the back panel would be glued and screwed into a good-sized rebate to help with the structure. Finally, I would take as much wind as possible by careful positioning of the hinges. If it all worked out as planned you would have to look very closely to notice that it wasn't true at all.

You may want to make your version of the cabinet from scratch, without having to solve the problems I was faced with – unless you have an old door lurking in the workshop.

Design and materials

Both the design and construction follow traditional lines, and it can be made suitable for either floor standing or wall mounting, with or without doors.

Size the carcass to suit your needs, but the sizes I have given will create a balanced cabinet, *see fig b*. If you're using oak, try to get hold of some quarter-sawn stock with good figure in it for the sides and top, it always

seems to look better.

Consider how many shelves are to be mounted. There are many systems available, but to my way of thinking 'library strip', or 'Tonk strip' is one of the best. It is strong, easy to install, has plenty of adjustment and looks the part. You can get it in either 'brassed' steel, brass or bronze. A cheaper 'lay on' version is available, but I don't think it looks quite as good.

If the cabinet is to be wall hung I would recommend buying or making flat thin metal corner plates to be added to the corners at the rear, so that the load on the wall fixings is passed back into the carcass rather than the relatively thin ply back panel.

The top is separate from, and overhangs, the carcass. It is screwed to the carcass from the inside, using oversized slotted holes to allow for timber movement.

The wall hung version requires the back edge of the top to finish flush with the rear of the cabinet. If floor standing I prefer to let

the top overhang at the rear to prevent small objects dropping down the back.

Should you wish to make a door, then there are many types of construction and style. Keep it simple and in keeping with the style of the cabinet. I don't deal with making the doors here, but there is some very good advice on their construction and tooling in Bob Adsett's articles in *TR8* and *13*.

Carcass construction

Select your best timber for the top and sides and prepare to thickness and width. Leave the boards over length so you have sufficient material for setting up both your router and dovetail jig. In any case, it's reassuring to have a bit extra since it's not unknown to have a glitch, such as cutting the pins in the wrong board!

Square off one end of each of the four carcass boards, set the dovetail jig and router, and take trial cuts until you're happy with the fit of the joint. Cut the two bottom right and

▼ Figure a Details of the rebate for the 'library/Tonk' shelving strip

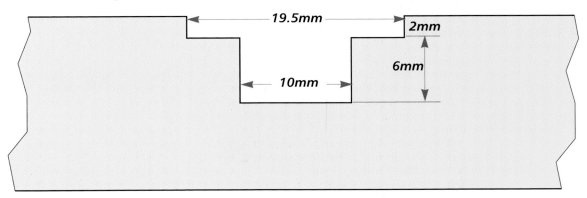

19.5mm

2mm

10mm

6mm

▲ While he is making the cabinet Bill gets his wife Betty to strip the door

▲ Cramp up the carcass with the door in position to make sure it fits, note the clingfilm to prevent the door adhering to the carcass. Cascamite for the dovetails and PVA for the biscuits

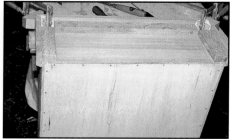

▲ The plinth was glued on with Titebond polyurethane. Components must be clamped as the glue expands, the excess is easily cleaned off when dry

▲ Masking tape on the carcass is easy to mark with the lock's mortice

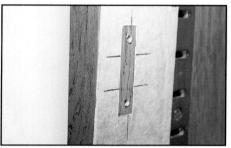

▲ The tape is then cut away to attach the striking plate

▲ The Tonk strip is easily fitted using a hole-centring bit

left-hand joints, mark and cut off, square and to length, both the sides and carcass top to the required height then rout the remaining top dovetails.

I chose to reduce the width of the carcass top by the thickness of the door so the door fits inside the carcass. If doing so, the top dovetails need to stop short at the front edge of the carcass sides.

I used a 'Tonk strip' with a cross-section of 2 by 19mm. Mark the positions of the strip and rout rebates so that the strip finishes flush with the interior surface of the carcass side boards. The rebate is in two steps to allow for the lug on the back of the shelf support.

Wealden Tool Company make a cutter specifically for this job, the T4430, but you can of course achieve the required rebate by using ordinary small diameter cutters, the T4430 makes it a lot easier and quicker.

Cut and file the four strips to length, ensuring that the distance from the bottom hanging slot to the end of each strip is identical, and mark the back of the strip 'top and bottom'. This should ensure the shelves end up level.

If you go for the 'brassed' steel strip don't be tempted to grind the strip to length with a cutting disc, the heat will melt the finish treatment and it could end up looking a mess.

Back

The 6mm oak-faced ply back requires a rebate to be cut into the back edges of the carcass. Go for a generous width of rebate, say 12mm, so that you have something to screw into, and just a little deeper than the ply thickness.

Sand, and if possible finish the interior faces, before gluing up the carcass. It's so much easier on the flat. Make up the ply back to snugly fit the rebated carcass, sand and finish, secure with suitably-sized brass countersink screws. If you use brass screws in oak then pilot drill the carcass or you stand a fair chance of the screws snapping on installation. The broken shank can be a pig to remove.

◀ The completed oak cabinet ready for finishing

▶ If the cabinet is to be floor standing insert a piece of oak in the top to tidy up, seen here on the top half only, for clarity

Plinth

Shape and sizes of the plinth should be to suit any existing furniture. If you intend to wall hang the cabinet then the bottom of the plinth should either be panelled in, left out, or replaced by a mirror image of the top. There are so many variations possible.

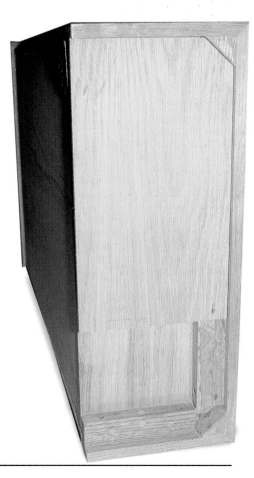

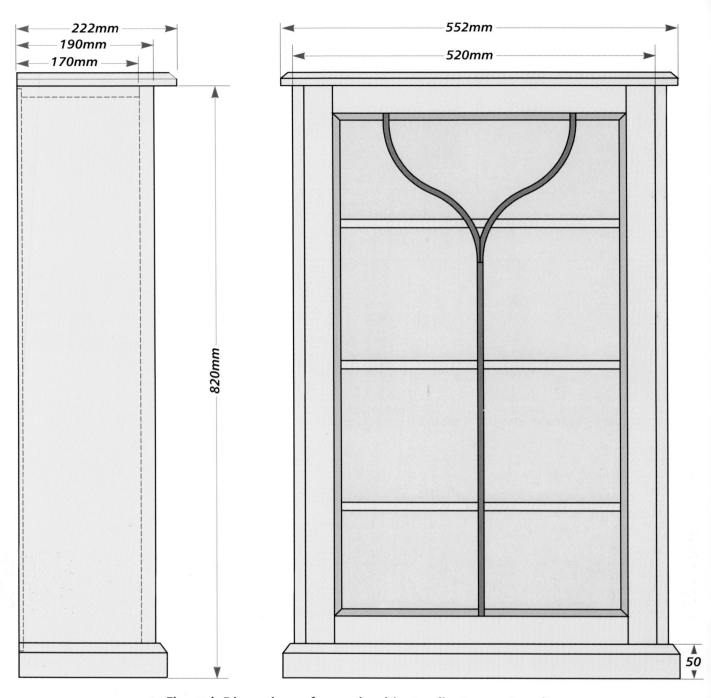

▲ *Figure b Dimensions of my oak cabinet, adjust yours to suit*

Top

As I mentioned earlier, this should be from your best-looking timber, and if in oak, hopefully with some figure in it. Prepare to size. I left an overhang of 16mm around the front sides and back to match the thickness of the plinth and the wall skirting board where it was to stand.

Rout a moulding onto the sides and front edge, again I went for something simple that matched existing furniture, using just the chamfer portion of a 25° panel fielding cutter, cutting until it looked right. Sand and finish.

Shelves

I like to keep these a little thinner than the carcass material, say 12mm, and about 30mm less in overall width so that there is plenty of clearance between the shelf edge

and the door glazing. Make up and finish to fit the carcass.

Finishing off

Screw the library strip into its rebates, ensuring it is the right way round. I find that a hinge centring bit, such as those sold by Axminster or Trend, are the right tools for the job, since they drill a pilot hole concentric with the countersink, and the screws then go in straight.

Complete the sanding and finishing of the carcass, mark off and drill, countersink, or slot the six off holes, oversize to allow for movement, through the carcass top. Position the cabinet top, back spot or pilot drill and screw the top to the carcass.

A suitable door of you choice can now be constructed to fit the completed cabinet, or the front can be left open, as you wish.

▼ *If wall mounted, fit metal corner brackets to take the load*

Peter Barton makes a home-grown medicine chest in which to hide his Night Nurse

Pharmacy fun

The cabinet described here is fairly small (Fig.l), since it was intended to fit into a limited space, but the method of construction could be used for one of almost any size. The project provides plenty of interesting router work in just a small amount of wood. A raised panel door is shown and this would have to be made on a router table. Some of the other work could also be done on a table, but if you don't have one then a plywood door could be fitted and all the rest of the work done with a lightweight hand-held router. This cabinet was made from pine and painted to match the bathroom, but it would look just as good in a furniture hardwood with a clear finish. It was built fairly shallow so that it wouldn't protrude too far past a washbasin, but if it was free-standing it could be given more capacity with greater depth back-to-front and all the other sizes adjusted to suit. Only common router cutters are needed.

Grooves for the housing joints might be made with a full-width cutter (Fig 2A) or by two passes with a narrower one (Fig 2B). An ogee moulding is suitable for edges (Fig 2C). A rebate cutter will let in the plywood back (Fig 2D). The grooves and mortices in the door frame are made with a straight cutter (Fig 2E). The door panel is raised with a moderate-size cutter (Fig 2F). If you want to make a finger grip on the door (Fig lA) a cove cutter is needed (Fig 2G), although a chamfer cutter might suffice.

Stash those sachets

1. Prepare wood for the sides, top and bottom. If you are starting with wide boards, arrange parts side by side and mark and cut grooves before separating (Photo 1). This would be a help when gripping for routing. The main and shelf joints are stopped housing (Fig 3A).

2. Mark top and bottom together (Fig 4A).

Leave cutting to length until after grooving.

3. Mark sides with their ends notched to match the grooves (Fig 4B).

4. Cut the joint grooves 9mm ($^3/8$in) deep. At the forward ends trim square with a chisel (Fig 3B and 4C) Photo 2.

5. Notch the sides to match, so rear edges will come flush (Fig 4D). Cut grooves for the shelves.

6. Cut top and bottom pieces to length and mould front and ends: on the grooved side on bottom and the opposite side on top.

7. Cut the rebates now to suit the plywood back (Fig 4C and D) or leave this until after assembly.

8. Clean up and sand all parts, then glue and cramp them. Check squareness.

9. If you didn't cut the rebates for the plywood back separately, go all around the insides of the rear edges with the rebate cutter and use a chisel to square the corners (Fig 3C).

Fig 1: Suggested sizes of cabinet

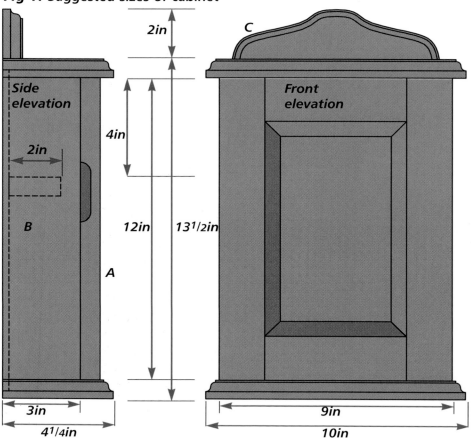

Side elevation

2in

Side elevation

2in

B

4in

12in   13½in

A

3in

4¼in

Front elevation

C

9in

10in

Prescription only

The door frame has mortice and tenon joints and the panel fits into grooves. The joints could have tenons cut on the crosswise parts, but the method suggested uses mortices both ways and inserted tenons.

14. Prepare wood for the frame. Cut the crosswise pieces to exact length between the sides, which can be left slightly too long until after assembly.

15. Try the panel cutter on a piece of scrap wood of the same thickness (Fig 2F). Try to leave no more than 8mm ($^5/_{16}$in) at

Photo 1 **Grooves cut with the simplest of guides and a clamp**

10. Make and fit the shelf (Fig lB). Take the sharpness off its front edges. See that the rear edge finishes level with the rebate (Photo 8).

11. Shape the decorative top (Fig lC and 5). It will be a help in securing with a cramp while shaping and moulding if this is done on a wide piece and cut off later. Mould the shaped edge and plane the bottom straight (Photo 3, 4, 5 and 6).

12. Glue the decorative top in place (Photo 7).

13. Fit the plywood back with glue and a few panel pins (Photo 9).

Photo 2 **After routing, square groove ends with chisel**

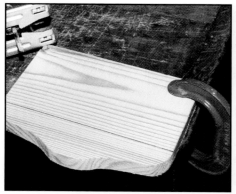

Photo 3 **Do the shaping on a wide piece of timber**

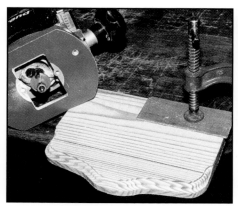

Photo 4 **Mould the edge entirely before cutting off**

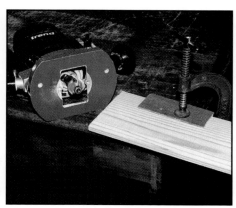

Photo 5 **Mould the top clamped over the bench end**

Photo 6 **Moulded parts ready for assembly**

the edge. If your cutter will not do this you'll have to thin the edges at the back of the panel. This controls the width of frame grooving (Photo 10).

16. Mark out the frame parts (Fig 6A).

17. Use a straight cutter that suits the panel edge to cut mortices 19mm (3/4in) in both directions at each corner (Fig 6B). To give a better bearing for the base of the router cramp wood alongside the part being cut.

18. Cut grooves for the panel, with the same cutter, full-length on top and bottom parts and into the mortices on the sides

Fig 2: Router cutters needed

Cutters for housings etc

A B

C **Ogee cutter for decorative top**

D **Rebater for back panel**

Cutter for door frame joints & grooves

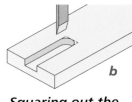

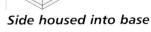
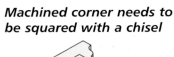
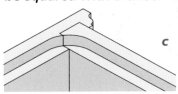

E

Finger pull cut with cove cutter

G

F **Ogee panel raiser for door**

Fig 3: Joint details

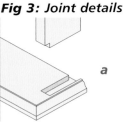

a

b

Squaring out the housings

Side housed into base

Machined corner needs to be squared with a chisel

c

Photo 7 **Assembled carcass with top being glued on**

Photo 8 **Rebating back of carcass requires a substantial bench clamp**

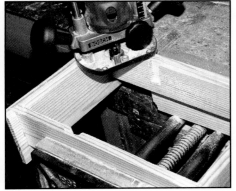

Photo 9 **Plywood back cut and ready to fit**

(Fig.6C).

19. Make a strip with rounded edges long enough to make the tenons and cut off four pieces (Fig 6D).

20. Cut the panel to a size that will make an easy fit. It should not reach the bottoms of the grooves.

21. Prepare the edges of the panel to fit the grooves (Fig 6E).

22. Try the joints. Do any necessary cleaning up and sanding.

23. Assemble the door, with glue in the joints, but it should be unnecessary to glue the panel (Photo 11).

Photo 10 **Grooving the door frame strip**

Photo 11 **The assembled door with both hinges attached**

Photo 12 **The final touch is to rout the finger grip**

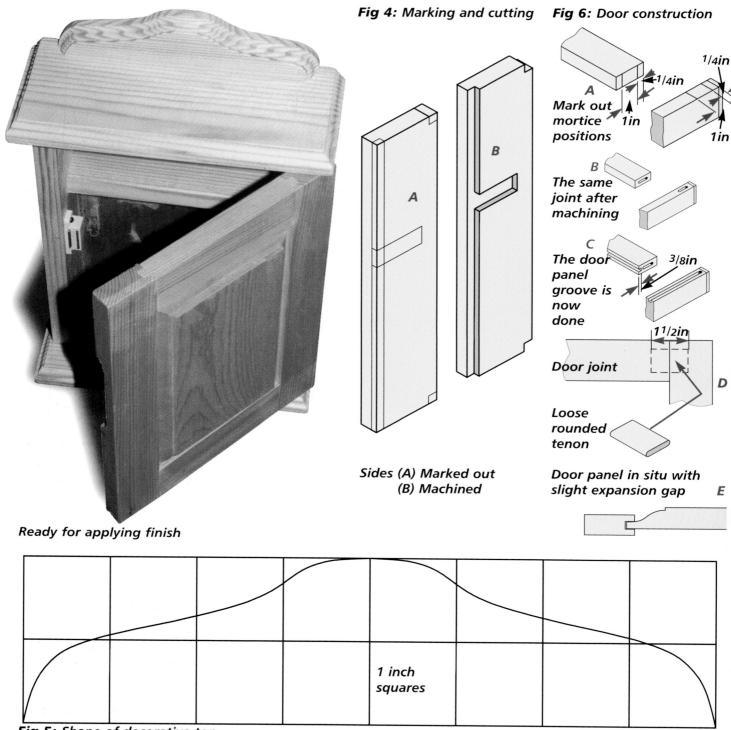

Fig 4: Marking and cutting

Fig 6: Door construction

A — Mark out mortice positions

1/4in

1/4in

1in

1in

B — The same joint after machining

C — The door panel groove is now done

3/8in

Door joint

1 1/2in

D

Loose rounded tenon

Door panel in situ with slight expansion gap

E

Sides (A) Marked out (B) Machined

Ready for applying finish

1 inch squares

Fig 5: Shape of decorative top

24. Ease the outside of the door, if necessary, to match the cabinet sides and to clear its top and bottom.

25. You could fit a knob or handle, but to avoid anything projecting, cut a finger grip (Fig 1A) using a cove cutter on the opening side for a length of about 75mm (3in).

26. Fit two hinges and a spring or magnetic catch.

27. Remove the metal fittings after a trial assembly, then apply the finish of your choice.

Cutting list

2 off sides	528 x 75 x 19mm (13 1/2 x 3 x 3/4in)
1 off top	250 x 107 x 19mm (10 x 4 1/4 x 3/4in)
1 off bottom	250 x 107 x 19mm (10 x 4 1/4 x 3/4in)
1 off top back	225 x 50 x 19mm (9 x 2 x 3/4in)
1 off shelf	240 x 50 x 19mm (9 1/2 x 2 x 3/4in)
2 off door sides	300 x 44 x 19mm (12 x 1 3/4 x 3/4in)
2 off door ends	138 x 44 x 19mm (5 1/2 x 1 3/4 x 3/4in)
1 off door panel	235 x 160 x 19mm (9 1/2 x 6 1/4 x 3/4in)
1 off back	325 x 210 x 6mm (12 3/4 x 8 1/4 x 1/4in plywood)

Bill Cain routs a saucepan rack that will leave your cupboards bare

Bill Cain

Saucy storage

S AUCEPANS stored on their base seem to take up a huge amount of cupboard space, so why not hang them from their handles? This saves space and can add to the overall kitchen decoration.

Design considerations

In designing a rack like this a number of factors have to be considered, in particular the weight it will carry.

The cast iron pans for which this rack was designed weigh some 12kgs in total. With the finished rack at about 9kgs, this means we are looking at something in the order of 22kgs by the time a few other bits and bobs are added.

A sound and strong structure is needed, and likewise the fixings that hold it to the wall also need to be substantial!

My design was sized to take four pans, ranging in size from 200 to 150mm (8in to 6in), plus a casserole dish of 225mm (9in) diameter. A full width drawer and a top shelf is included. The overall dimensions come out at 600mm wide by 267mm deep by 760mm high (24 by 10½ by 30in).

I have used a number of construction techniques which employ various bits of kit and cutters, much of which was kindly loaned by Trend and Axminster Power Tool Centre.

"Quebec yellow pine works easily and finishes well"

Tooling up

- Lock mitre cutter
- Bearing guided moulding cutter
- Bearing guided straight cutter
- Straight cutter
- Cove cutter
- Slotting cutter
- Bearing guided rebate cutter
- Dovetail cutter
- Upcut spiral cutter
- Downcut spiral cutter

▲ **Keep your saucepans tidy and accessible**

▲ *I joined the boards together with a lock mitre to make them wide enough for the project*

▲ *Cut the dovetail joints on the sides and bottom*

Material selection

The material chosen, 'Quebec' yellow pine, (*Pinus strobus*), also known as 'Weymouth' or 'soft' pine, is light both in weight and colour, works easily and finishes well.

Your choice of timber, final colouring, sizing and edge mouldings etc. really depend on pan sizes and any pieces of kitchen furniture which it may have to blend in with.

▼ *Dimensions of side panels*

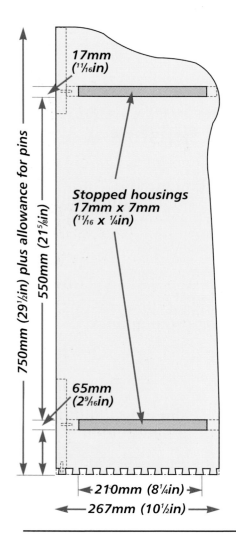

17mm
(¹¹/₁₆in)

Stopped housings
17mm x 7mm
(¹¹/₁₆ x ¼in)

65mm
(2⁹/₁₆in)

750mm (29½in) plus allowance for pins

550mm (21⁵/₈in)

◄ 210mm (8¼in) ►

◄ 267mm (10½in) ►

I bought the timber rough sawn, so control of sizes and squareness was down to me. With ready prepared timber you may have to juggle the dimensions slightly, and judging from some of the prepared timber I have seen for sale, some work will be needed to ensure that boards are true, square, and of a constant, identical thickness.

"With ready prepared timber you may have to juggle the dimensions slightly"

Carcass construction

The timber I used wasn't wide enough for the sides, bottom and two shelves, so I had to join pieces together to achieve the width required. Prepare the stock ensuring that lengthwise faces to be jointed are true and square.

My choice for this task was the lock mitre joint, as it is quick to cut, has plenty

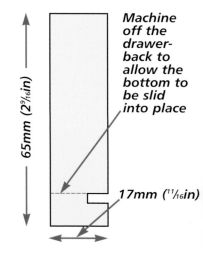

Machine off the drawer-back to allow the bottom to be slid into place

65mm (2⁹/₁₆in)

17mm (¹¹/₁₆in)

▲ *Cross-section of drawer sides, back and front*

of glue area and produces a strong accurate joint with very little cleaning up required.

For gluing I used Titebond polyurethane. This has a very short cure time of about four hours, and boards jointed in the morning were dovetailed in the afternoon. When dry, cut and finish to width all boards.

Clamp the sides back-to-back to make sure the housings line up and there is a right and left-hand version

▲ Decide on a design for the side's shape and cut the pieces slightly oversize

▲ With a thin template, rout the side to a final shape

▲ Apply the edge moulding to all components that require it

Side panels and bottom

Mark out and cut the bottom to the finished length, then square off one end of each side panel and cut the dovetails.

If using a dovetail jig to cut the dovetails, as I did, then it is almost certain that when you apply a decent size moulding to the edge of the component you will cut back into the tails or sockets in some way. It's not a real problem but the result can sometimes look a bit odd.

With the sides cramped back-edge to back-edge, inside faces up, mark out and rout all the stopped housing joints for the shelves in one operation to ensure both sides are identically spaced.

Top and bottom shelves

Mark out and cut the top and bottom shelves to length, make sure they include the depth of the housings they will fit into. Cut notches in the back and front ends of the shelves to create tongues that match the housing lengths. To make fitting together easier, chamfer the tongue ends slightly so they enter their housings without damage.

The top and bottom back panels are fixed to both the shelves and the carcass sides, so measure them and cut to length. They are the components that take the weight, so drill and countersink a couple of holes in each for wall hangings.

Dry assembly

Dry assemble all the above parts, adjust fits as required, and try to use the same degree of cramping pressure that will be used when gluing up.

Ensure that the structure is true and square in all planes, and mark all parts so they go back together in their 'as fitted' positions.

While it is assembled, mark out the positions of the rebates required in the back faces to accept the 3mm (⅛in) thick hardboard back panel, and disassemble.

This thin rear panel could be made from solid timber or even left out. I have included it in order to prevent damage to the wall coverings when pans are removed or replaced, and it's easy to wipe clean.

Biscuit joints and rebates

Mark out the positions and cut the biscuit slots, (size '10' biscuits), in the ends of the top and bottom back panels, bottom face of the bottom back panel, and inside rear faces of the sides and bottom panel. You will need 13 biscuits in all.

For some time now for cutting biscuit joints I have used a Trend slotting cutter set and Elu 117E router inverted in an Elu table, a combination that works well. However, when a panel's narrow edge is face down on the table a little extra care is required.

For safety, cramp the work to a thick block, or better still an angle plate, to prevent the work from tipping when presenting it to the cutter.

Rout the rebates for the hardboard back panel in the top and bottom back panels and the carcass sides, which will need the rounded corners of the rebate cut square with a chisel.

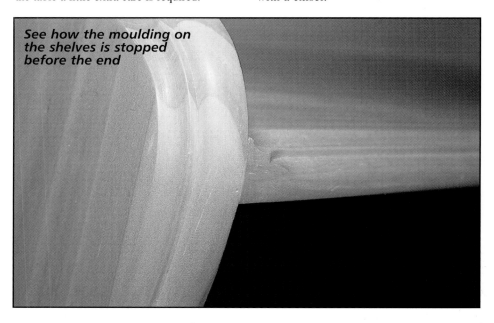

See how the moulding on the shelves is stopped before the end

Cutting list

17mm thick pine

2off	sides	267 by 750 plus allowance for dovetail pins
1off	bottom	600 by 267
1off	hanging rail	566 by 80
2off	top and bottom shelves	580 by 566
2off	top and bottom panel	566 by 150
1off	lid rack base	275 by 80
2off	drawer sides	65 by 216 plus allowance for dovetail pins
2off	drawer front and back	65 by 566

3mm (⅛in) thick white faced hardboard

1off	back panel	586 by 470
1off	drawer bottom	544 by 239

12.7mm dowels

8off	lid rack	127

All sizes in millimetres

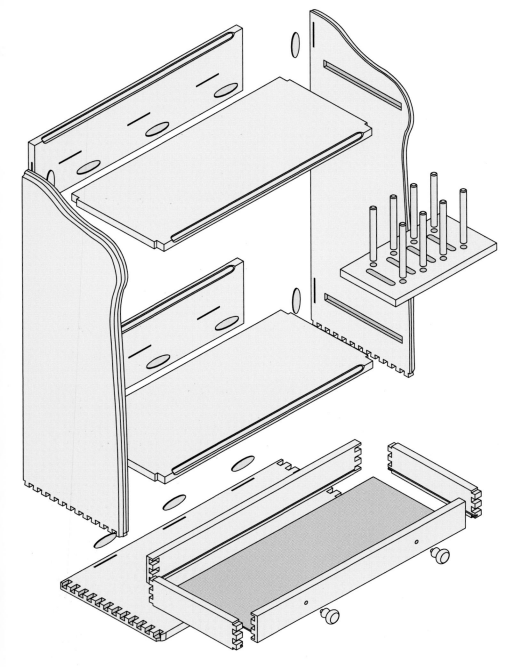

▲ *Screw the lid rack in place*

Profiling the side panels

Mark out your selected profile onto 6mm (¼in) MDF, this could be a design to match other units in the kitchen or a free-form design of your choice. Cut and finish to shape for use as a routing template.

Transfer the template shape to the side panels then bandsaw, jigsaw or otherwise cut the side panels to shape, but oversize, leaving about 1.5mm (¹⁄₁₆in) to be removed by routing.

Fix the template to the work with double sided carpet tape and profile rout both the side panels.

Decorative mouldings

Mould the top and bottom inside edges of the top back panel, the top inside edge of the bottom back panel, and the front top edges of the top and bottom shelves.

I used a Trend back-to-back bench clamp to secure the work whilst freehand routing these mouldings. I was impressed by this tool's holding ability, and if purchasing I would go for the 50in long version.

Leave the side panel mouldings until the carcass is finally glued and assembled.

Carcass assembly

As always this is where the 'fun' starts, never enough time, cramps or hands! Finish sand all parts, taking care not to sand away the crisp edges of mouldings, and get everything

▲ *Exploded view of the saucepan rack*

▼ *Set up the slotting cutter for routing biscuit slots*

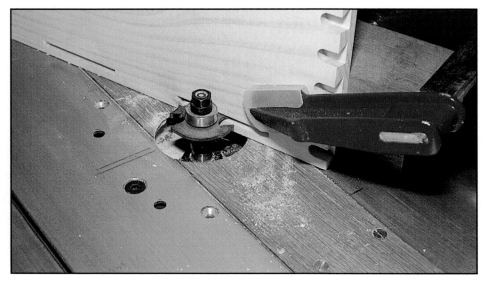

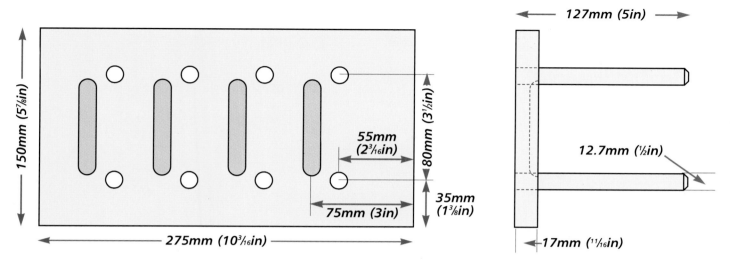

150mm (5⅞in)

275mm (10³⁄₁₆in)

55mm (2³⁄₁₆in)

75mm (3in)

80mm (3½in)

35mm (1⅜in)

127mm (5in)

12.7mm (½in)

17mm (¹¹⁄₁₆in)

▼ The fully finished saucepan rack just needs fixing to the wall

ready and available for gluing. There are quite a few surfaces and biscuits to come together, so speed and an 'plan of action' are essential.

I had assistance, and a plan, so things were looking good.

I glued up all the components with PVA, other than one side panel. Then I cramped up all parts including the unglued side panel, got the structure square and then quickly removed the glue-free panel, glued it, replaced it and cramped back up, ensuring the completed structure was true and square in all planes.

With 3.5mm x 35mm countersunk screws, fix the top and bottom back panels into the edge of the top and bottom shelves to hold them securely in place.

The last job was to clean up and rout the decorative moulding around both side panels.

Drawer and rack

The drawer is made in a conventional manner to fit the carcass. I like to make drawers so that they only just enter, and then progressively fit them to size using a very sharp plane, you can always remove material, putting it back is difficult!

As to construction, prepare stock to size, cut the dovetail joints on the front, back and sides, then rout the groove in them for the drawer bottom.

Glue up with PVA, and cramp very lightly, just sufficient to squeeze the glue, and ensure all is square and true.

Cut off the bottom edge of the back to the top of the groove by routing so the bottom panel can be slid into place. Cut the bottom panel to size and sand, plane or rout a slight chamfer on its underside to make it easier to slide in the grooves. Slide it into the drawer structure and secure it to the back with small screws, staples or pins.

Cut the pieces of wood for the saucepan hanging rail and lid storage rack. Screw hooks in the hanging rail and then screw it to the underside of the top shelf. Rout shallow grooves in the lid rack with a cove cutter and place the dowels in positions to suit your lid sizes.

Final finishing

'Quebec' pine has a natural 'soft' feel and look to it, and the final finish really depends on what you want. I chose several coats of Danish Oil followed by soft wax.

Once all finishing is complete, the hanging rail or lid storage can be screwed into place with 4.5mm x 25mm countersunk screws.

Attach the rear hardboard panel by whatever means you chose, I stapled mine, but if you feel like it a few screws will do the same job.

Make up and fit the rear panel, which like the drawer bottom can be secured by a variety of methods.

Finally, the drawer handles are fitted and the unit is ready to be mounted in position on the wall.

Peter Spiteri creates a cabinet to store his wine-making paraphernalia

Open all hours

Since the dawn of time man has found ways of making alcohol. When you consider you can ferment just about anything, it's not surprising there are so many varieties of falling-down water. I've been a keen winemaker for several years but have never seen anything that was specifically tailored to house all the winemaker's kit. My first thoughts were to convert a small oak barrel, but these are few and far between, so I eventually decided on a basic cabinet in ordinary softwood that could be reproduced easily by anyone with basic routering skills.

You'll need all the items in the box below, but do spend a bit of time if possible selecting the best pieces of 230mm x 25mm (9 x 1in) PAR available; timber of this width is often bowed, so have a good sort through the stock.

Brew up

Square off and cut the two sides to the dimensions on plan A. Lightly mark off the 10mm rebates for the shelves, and the 20mm rebate for the top. Mark off the rebate for the 8mm parting bead and then mark the left and right sides, because you want a mirror image of each one, not two left or vice versa! Set

your router to cut to a depth of 10mm using a 10mm two flute cutter. You are now ready to cut the three grooves needed on each panel, remembering that only one of these goes the full width! I used a piece of batten clamped at the right setting to guide the straight edge on the router baseplate. Square off the ends with your chisel.

While your cutter's still in, reset it to cut the rebate that receives the back of the unit. I chose 4mm ply for this. You need to set your cutter to give a depth of 4mm and a width of 10mm. Router along the entire edge from top to bottom, making sure you do the inside edge. Change your bit to a 22mm two flute cutter as you are now ready to router the top rebate. You will need to set your router to cut to a depth of 10mm and to the full 20mm

width. Run the router along the top edge of both side panels. The last piece of routing needed now is the rebate to receive the parting bead. For this you will need an 8mm two flute cutter, set to a depth of 10mm, and a guide batten to keep the router on a true course. This is only a small cut and will once again have to be finished with a chisel. Once this last step has been completed you can put the two sides safely aside until the shelves are completed.

Top shelf optics

Cut all four pieces from your 230mm x 25mm (9 x 1in) PAR as per diagram. To avoid confusion when it comes to assembling the unit, mark each shelf according to its finished position, i.e. top, half shelf, threequarter shelf and bottom.

Materials

3 m 230mm x 25mm PAR
3 m 75mm x 25mm PAR
1 m 75mm ogee architrave
1 length of 8mm x 20mm pine hockey (used for drawer lipping)
1 length of 8.5mm x 21mm pine decorative moulding

1 610mm x 610mm x 4mm ply/hardboard
1 small and 1 medium wooden knob
50mm cupboard hinges
1 roller catch
3 12mm tool clips
1 38mm tool clip (plastic coated)
610mm x 8mm parting bead

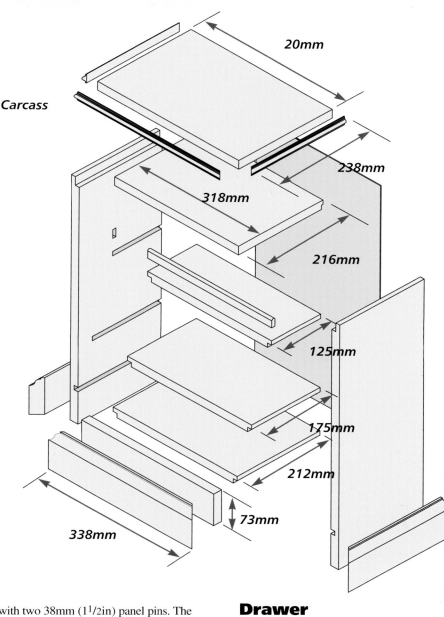

Carcass

20mm

238mm

318mm

216mm

125mm

175mm

212mm

73mm

338mm

There is only a small difference between the top and bottom shelf so make sure you're clear which is which. On the half, three-quarter and bottom shelf, a 10mm rebate should be put on both ends of each piece. I used my 22mm cutter for this and ended up with a 10mm x 10mm 'tongue'. Then rebate the top on the back edge to receive the plywood back. The cutter should be reset to give a cut of 4mm deep and 10mm wide. Once you've done this and cut your parting bead to length, assembly can begin.

Grape & grain

Try a dry-run assembly first, and sand off any loose swarf or marks left from marking out. Even when assembled dry you should find the unit becomes 'solid' and ready to be glued up permanently. You can use any PVA wood glue or equivalent. Place one side panel flat with rebates facing upwards. Lightly glue all grooves and shelves on one end. Fit into their respective positions and then repeat for the other side, being careful not to get glue everywhere when lowering the second side onto the shelves. Don't forget to include the parting bead. Gently clamp with sash clamps and leave overnight after clearing off any surplus glue and checking the unit for squareness. After releasing the clamps, fit the spacer piece and the ogee architrave to the base of the unit. Cut a piece of 20mm timber to the dimensions given and fit in position so that it is 10mm below the bottom shelf. Lightly glue and fix each end

with two 38mm (1¹/2in) panel pins. The architrave should now be mitred to fit the front and sides and these pieces can be screwed in position with two 32mm (1¹/4in) No.8 screws in each piece, screwed from behind the spacer piece and side panels. The decorative top can now be cut to size and once again the front and sides were faced with the remainder of the 21mm decorative moulding. You should end up with an overhang of approximately 16mm at the sides, and 26mm at the front. You will need to biscuit joint two pieces of timber together to achieve the necessary width. When you've routered the groove on both pieces, cut your ply or similar to be approximately 1mm smaller than the overall width. Glue the surfaces together and leave clamped overnight. When dry, cut to size and clean up. When the mouldings have been cut, fix them in position with a few dabs of PVA and two moulding pins each. You will need to plane or sand off any excess on the mouldings to become flush. Once the top's in position it can be permanently fixed with four 32mm (1¹/4in) No.8 screws from the inside of the unit, near each corner.

Drawer

The drawer opening should measure 300mm x 81mm. Refer to the drawings and cut your timber from the remnants of the 230mm x 25mm (9 x 1in) - the base of the drawer can be either 4mm ply or hardboard. Set your router with a 4mm two flute cutter to a cut depth of 6mm, which in turn needs to be 6mm from the bottom of the timber. When all four pieces have been grooved, you'll need to get your 22mm cutter ready to do the rebates on the front and rear pieces. Set the cutter to a cut depth of 10mm and the full width of 20mm. Rebate both ends of the front and rear pieces and you are now ready to assemble the drawer. There's no real need to glue the base, but the sides do need gluing to the rebate and clamped while drying. While you're waiting, find a piece of scrap timber so you can set your 22mm cutter ready for the lipping. You want to achieve a flush fit of the lipping on all four sides of the front. I ended up with a depth of 4mm and a width of 16mm, but do double check as I feel this item may vary from area to area. Also make sure you mark the four sides which are to receive the

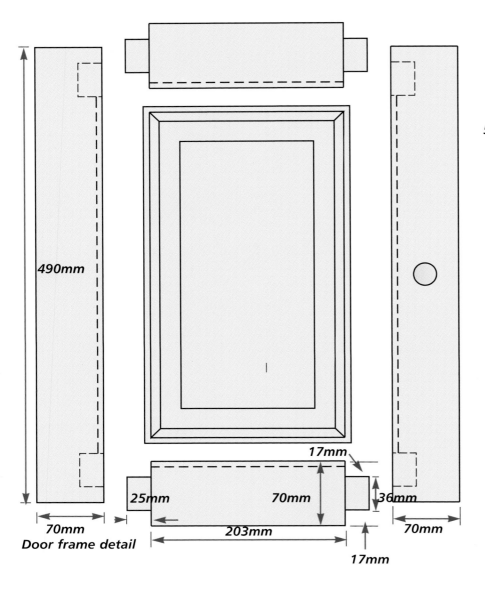

Door frame detail

490mm

17mm

25mm 70mm 36mm

203mm

70mm 70mm

17mm

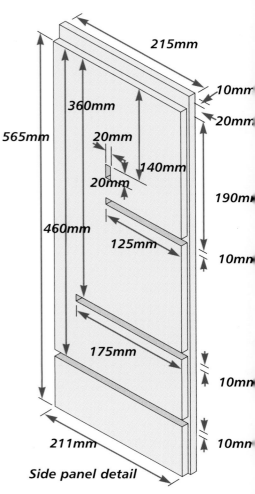

215mm

10mm

20mm

360mm

20mm

140mm

565mm

20mm

190mm

460mm

125mm

10mm

175mm

10mm

211mm

10mm

Side panel detail

lipping in bold pen or pencil as there are 14 directions in which to go wrong! Also, at this stage I decided it would look nice to wax the unit and show off the lipping. Simply glue the lippings in position once you're happy they fit well.

Shown the door

Cut all pieces as per plan from 75mm x 25mm (3 x 1in) and the panel piece from 230mm x 25mm (9 x 1in). On the door frame I used a blind mortice and tenon joint, with the panel stepped and fitted into the framework with a rebate, all of which is done with the router. Mark out your sides, top and bottom for the mortice and tenons.To do the mortice first fit an 8mm two flute cutter and set the depth for 25mm. Set this on the guide bar so that there's 6mm on both sides of the mortice. Place both sides together and firmly clamp them in a workmate or vice, making sure the edges are flush and there's enough clearance all round to manoeuvre the router. With all four mortices showing, you can now plunge to achieve the required depth. When this is done just clean up the mortices with a chisel. The tenons require a 22mm cutter. Having marked them out, cut first using a tenon saw round the four faces, but only to a maximum depth of 6mm .

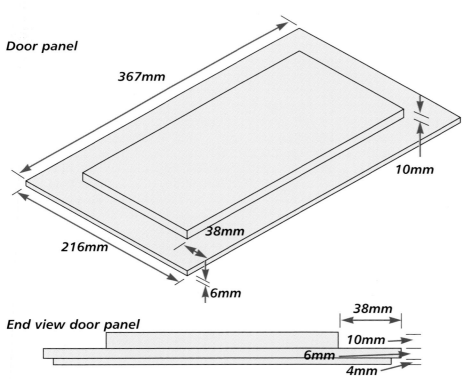

Door panel

367mm

10mm

38mm

216mm

6mm

End view door panel

38mm

10mm

6mm

4mm

Drawer

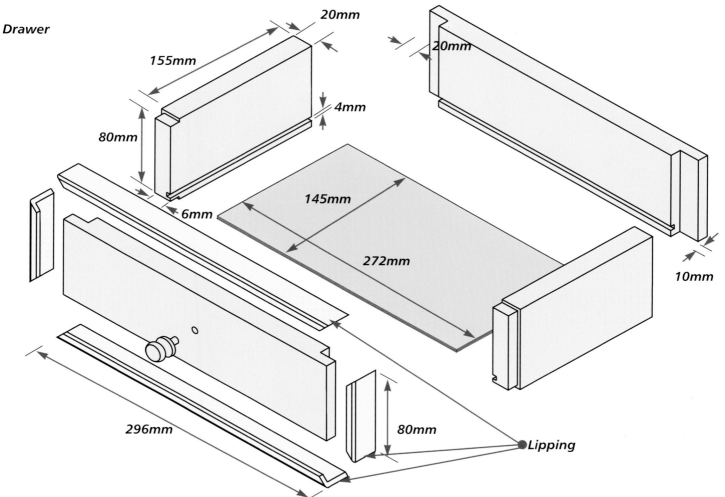

155mm
20mm
80mm
4mm
20mm
6mm
145mm
272mm
10mm
296mm
80mm
Lipping

This will give a clean edge that your cutter will stop at, and you'll need to set this to cut a depth of 6mm. Set the guide bar so that the cut only goes to the line, and cut all four tenons. Remove the remaining timber with a tenon saw to give the same dimensions as per diagram. Make sure that everything's tight and that the surfaces are flush. When the frame is assembled (dry), mark the internal edges as these will now be grooved to receive the panel. Dismantle the frame and mark out your 6mm groove, noting that it is off centre to allow for the stepped panel. Set your cutter to give a depth of 6mm and then your guide bar to 10mm. You should have 10/6/4mm marked out clearly and you can then router these four edges to give the finished measurements.

The frame can be put aside for now as you need to make the panel. This is made from 230mm x 25mm (9 x 1in) PAR and the finished size is 211mm x 30mm (8^{7}/16in x 13/16in), so let's work metric! You only need to cut the length of the panel as the width should be correct, but do double check as timber can vary from yard to yard. Set your 22mm cutter to give a maximum depth of 10mm. Then set your guide bar to give a cut of 20mm. Choose the best face to the front, and then router all four edges. Having done this you need to reset the guide bar to give a

total width of 38mm and once again cut all four edges. Spend a bit of time getting yourself comfortable for this part of the operation, because if you waver on this second cut you'll end up with different depths of cut. Rebate with a sharpened 38mm (1^{1}/2in) chisel held upright, then pulled back along the rebate. Sand to finish off.

Next reset your cutter to give a depth of 4mm and your guide bar to give a width of 6mm. Turn the panel over and rebate all four edges. Fit the panel to the frame and glue, clamp and check for squareness. When dry, offer up to your unit and plane as required to give an accurate fit all round. The small shelf was simply made from 200mm of 32mm x 8mm timber and then mitred round the outside edge with a parting bead. To fix to the door, simply measure up from the bottom 115mm and centralise to the width of the door. Glue and leave overnight. I used Cascamite for this but any PVA-based adhesive will do. The last fittings on the door are the mouldings and you will need to mitre these to the required size, making sure you have a snug fit. To hang the door, position the hinges 75mm from both the top and bottom. Mark and fix the hinges, but only put one screw in the bottom hinge. Offer the door up to the unit, align it all round and mark the hinge positions. Unscrew the bottom hinge,

line up on the marks and mark the screw holes. Permanently fit the hinge back on the door, offer it up and screw the hinges home. Next fit the roller catch threequarters up the inside edge. With the back off, it's easy to align the catchplate on the door.

Last orders

I wanted a stripped pine look, and find that wax gives an 'older' appearance on new timber. Apply with either a rag, brush or 000 steel wool, leave for a few hours and then buff off with a clean rag. Don't leave it on overnight as it can be a pig to remove the excess once it's hardened. After buffing I fitted the door mouldings with a few dabs of adhesive. The medium knob on the door is fitted in the middle of the door stile, and halfway up. Likewise, the small knob on the drawer is fitted centrally. The three 12mm (1/2in) tool clips can be positioned anywhere within the meatier part of the door panel.

CUTTERS USED
4mm Two flute
6mm Two flute
8mm Two flute
10mm Two flute
22mm Two flute

SPICY

Alan Parry tidies up with a practical spice shelf

A friend that loves cooking kept all her spice jars in a cardboard box and frequently found stocks depleted because they were hidden away. The remedy was a decent sized shelf incorporating a few features to aid the cook.

After sketching some ideas the final design consisted of five shelves to carry about 40 jars; two small drawers to hold odds and ends; a rail to hang drying spices and a clock.

materials used

The project is mainly made using 70 x 14mm (2³/4 x ⁵/8in) PAR pine and 95 x 7mm (3³/4 x ¹/4in) TG&V cladding boards available from DIY stores and quality timber merchants. They usually come wrapped in polythene. The drawer bottoms are 2mm (⁵/64in) thick ply and the rail is made from 16mm (³/8in) diameter dowel. You can adjust the timber dimensions to suit the materials you have available. In this case, Titebond was used to glue the parts together but any good PVA will do.

blackboard

I wanted full width TG&V boards to show so they controlled the width of the rack.

Cut the five boards just over 1mm in length and smooth the bottom edges with a medium grit abrasive paper. Mark and cut out the semicircles (**photo 1**) then smooth with abrasive paper wrapped around a thick dowel such as a

Photo 1 Mark and cut out semi-circles...   **Photo 2** ...then cut out the curves   **Photo 3** Moulding the TG&V board

broom handle. Make any necessary adjustments and glue the boards together ensuring the sides are square to the bottom. When dry, remove the tongue from one end board and smooth the edge.

making sides

Cut the two sides to length and cut the top edge at 45 degrees. A hand mitre saw is ideal for cutting angles accurately. The next step is to cut out the curves, using the grid paper as a guide mark (see **photo 2**). A coping saw is an ideal tool for making small cuts on thin wood.

Place both sides together and mark the shelf positions using a marking knife and try square. On the waste side saw to a depth of 4mm (1/16in) and remove the waste side, with a very sharp chisel. Clean the housings with either a hand router or abrasive paper. The use of an electric router and a suitable cutter enables you to make the housings quickly and cleanly. The final item on the sides is to bore the 16mm (5/8in) diameter holes for the hanging rail. A piece of scrap clamped to the underside will ensure a clean cut as the bit breaks out.

shelves and cover strip

Cut the five shelves to length and check that they fit into their respective housings, making any adjustments if necessary. The drawer support shelf is made with two lengths of 70 x 14mm (23/4 x 5/8in) PAR glued together and cut to size once dry.

The cover strip is made from TG&V boarding and moulded with a round file every 40mm (15/8in) or so (see **photo 3**). A cover strip hides, to joint between the backboard and underside of the capping pieces. You can buy a strip ready moulded or leave it plain, depending on your preference.

capping & movement holder

The capping movement holders are wider than the sides and made with three 700mm (275/8in) lengths of 70 x 40mm (23/4 x 5/8in) PAR glued together to create a piece which totals 210mm (81/4in) wide. An ordinary rubbed joint will be satisfactory, so long as the piece is kept flat while it dries. From this piece the two caps and movement holder can be cut to size. As already mentioned, a mitre saw is ideal for cutting the ends and 'apex' of the capping at 45 degrees.

Glue the cap pieces together, holding them with a mitre clamp until dry (**photo 4**). End grain joints should be sealed with diluted PVA before gluing as to prevent the glue being drawn away from the joint and weakening it. A Hechinger W4 movement with a medium length spindle is ideal for this shelf. Use the movement as a guide to rout or chisel out the recess (**photo 5**). Any slight overcut with regard to depth can be made-up with plastic washers or similar packing. It's very important that the holder fits the recess correctly before gluing it into position, as it can not be adjusted once put in place.

putting it together

Before starting to assemble the shelf, check that the parts go together correctly and, if not, make the necessary adjustments. Lightly rub over the surfaces with a fine abrasive paper and ensure that you have enough clamps and adhesive. Apply glue to the housings and insert the shelves ensuring they project beyond the sides at the front, allowing space for the backboard to fit in the rear. Once the glue has dried, pin and glue the backboard in position.

Cut the top of the backboard using the capping piece as a guide (**photo 6**). Make and fit two 'eaves' and one 'apex' glue block. Glue and pin the capping in position, making sure it's exactly central, and glue in the movement cover holder. Cut the dowel rail to length and make two end caps to cover the holes (**photo 7**). The caps are made from two thin slices of broom handle slightly rounded around the circumference. Lastly, cut and fit the division piece between the drawers and the moulding cover strips.

making the drawers

The drawer dimensions given in the cutting list are merely a guide and you'll have to adjust them to suit the size of your drawer opening.

Cut the parts to size and make a groove in the front and side pieces for the plywood bottom (**photo 8**). I made the grooves with a tenon saw followed by rubbing a piece of folded abrasive paper along the cut. Drill the 4mm (1/16in) diameter dowel holes in the front piece and sides, using a dowel jig or locating pins. Glue the sides to the front (**photo 9**), slide in the base (**photo 10**), and then pin and glue the back in position (**photo 11**). Clamp until dry (**photo 12**). Finally, add the pulls or knobs to suit.

fitting the clock

Insert the movement and tighten the locking nut, press the self-adhering dial in place checking the 12 and 6 are truly vertical. To prevent damaging the hands it's best to fit them after the finishing has been completed.

finishing

Poor finishing can very easily ruin a good piece of woodwork. To ensure this does not happen, rub the piece over with a fine abrasive paper and be sure to fill any pinholes and unwanted blemishes. Apply two coats of satin varnish to seal the surfaces. But remember that staining or any other finish is optional to suit the room the shelf is to reside.

Photo 4 A mitre clamp does the job

Photo 5 Rout out recess

Photo 6 Cutting the backboard

Photo 7 Neat end caps cover rail ends

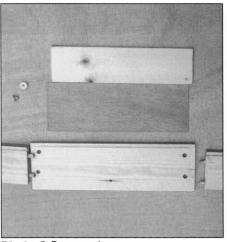

Photo 8 Drawer pieces

Photo 9 Glue sides to drawer front

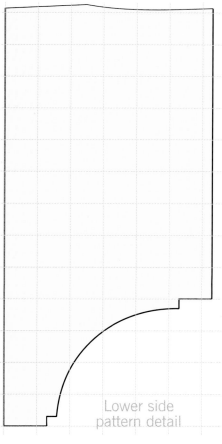

Lower side
pattern detail

Drawer construction

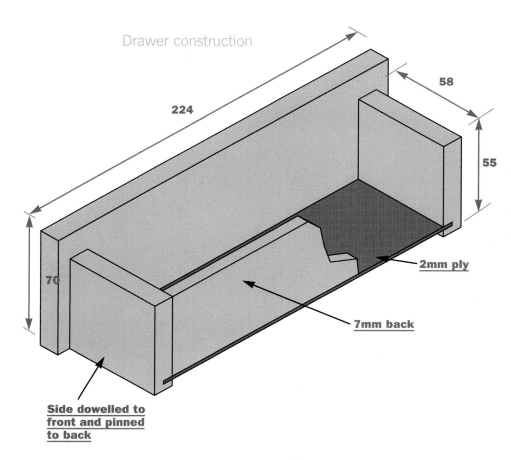

224

58

55

70

2mm ply

7mm back

Side dowelled to front and pinned to back

Photo 10 Slide in drawer base.

Photo 12 Clamp drawers until dry

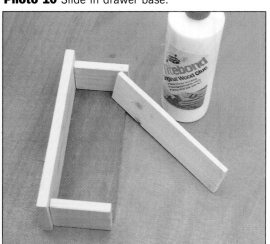

Photo 11 Complete assembly

Cutting List (All in mm)				
Part	**No**	**L**	**W**	**T**
Side	2	780	70	12
Drawer shelf	1	449	82	12
Spice shelves	5	449	70	12
Division piece	1	70	58	12
Capping	2	400	95	12
Movement holder	1	220	110	12
Dowel rail	1	465	16mm diameter	
Cover pieces	2	28mm diameter		5
Backboard	1	1000	441	7
Made from five TG&V boards				
Drawer front	2	224	70	12
Drawer side	4	68	55	12
Drawer back	2	188	50	7
Drawer bottom	2	194	71	12
Glue blocks	3	To suit eaves & apex location		

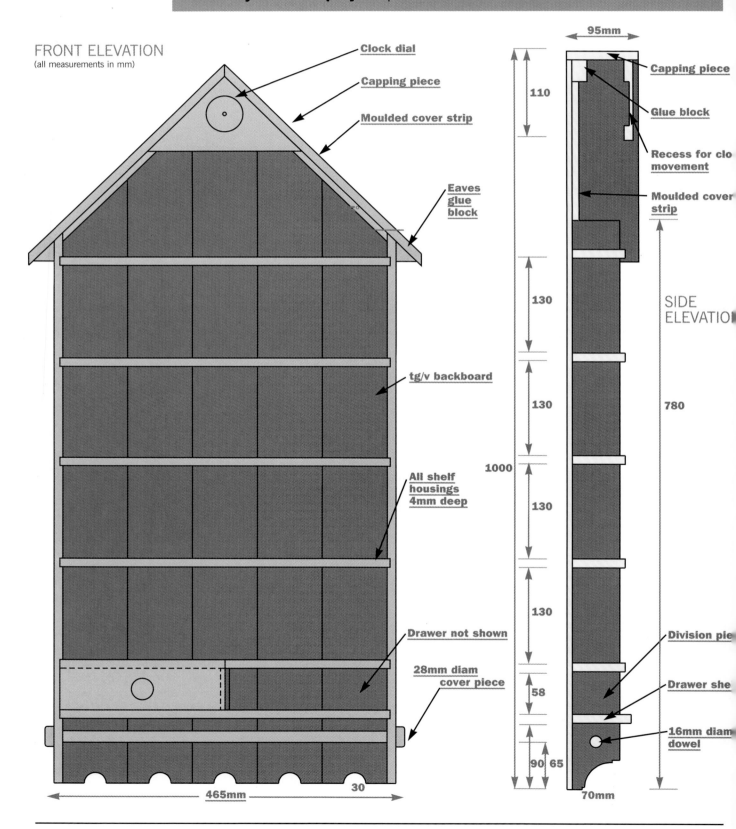

FRONT ELEVATION
(all measurements in mm)

Clock dial

Capping piece

Moulded cover strip

Eaves glue block

tg/v backboard

All shelf housings 4mm deep

Drawer not shown

28mm diam cover piece

465mm · 30

110 · 130 · 130 · 130 · 130 · 58 · 90 · 65 · 1000

SIDE ELEVATION

95mm

Capping piece

Glue block

Recess for clock movement

Moulded cover strip

780

Division piece

Drawer shelf

16mm diam dowel

70mm

MAKER

Terry Lawrence

Terry Lawrence likes to keep tidy by making boxes for his bits and bobs

Get boxed!

I HAVE always been interested in making boxes, but wanted to make something a little different from commercially available ones.

This is one of the simplest designs with proper joints; comb or finger joints with a rebated lid and base.

Once set up, you can make the carcass in an hour or so, and then devote a little more time to embellishment; using paint,

pyrography, stain, or a covering of cloth, leather or veneer.

I made a plywood carcass, the exterior veneered with dark harewood. As extras, I inlaid home-made coloured bandings into the veneer, and a lining of rich yellow leather.

Carcass

I selected classic 3:2:1 proportions for the box, although these are modified a little,

when the lid is separated from the base.

The overall dimensions are 300 by 200 by 100mm (11¹³⁄₁₆ by 7⅞ by 4in), the height reducing to 94mm (3¹¹⁄₁₆in) after separating the lid with the ¼in cutter.

Method

As many of you will have different set-ups to me, modify my methods to suit your particular equipment.

▼*An attractive box, veneered and lined*

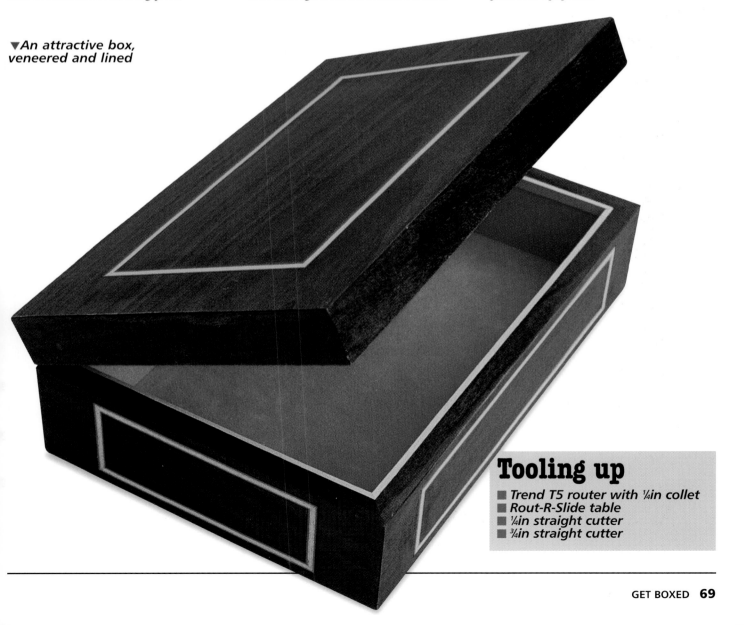

Tooling up

■ *Trend T5 router with ¼in collet*
■ *Rout-R-Slide table*
■ *¼in straight cutter*
■ *¾in straight cutter*

Cutting a comb joint on a Rout-R-Slide table

Cut your joints with your router, either by the method I have used, with a dovetail jig, or perhaps with the comb jointing jig designed by Bob Wearing, *see TR13*.

Dimension the 10 or 12mm (⅜ or ½in) ply components to the sizes given, *see Cutting list*. Don't go any thinner than 10mm (⅜in) though; you will need the strength to combat possible warping of the 6mm (¼in) ply lid and base panels.

All ply warps a bit, and while MDF would be more stable, it won't joint cleanly in thinner dimensions.

"Many of you will have different set-ups to me, so modify my methods to suit your particular equipment"

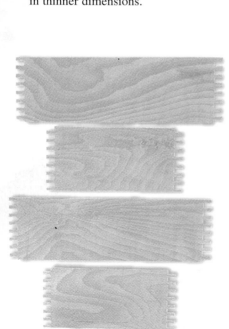

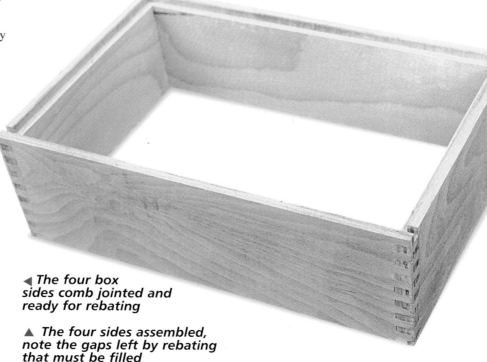

◄ The four box sides comb jointed and ready for rebating

▲ The four sides assembled, note the gaps left by rebating that must be filled

With the bottom fitted, start separating the lid

Slots

If you are fortunate to own a Rout-R-Slide table, as I am, make a fence from ¾in thick timber then cut a slot in it with the ¼in cutter, set at a suitable height for the joint. Plug this slot with a small piece of timber stub of the exact width, projecting forward a little. This will be the locater for creating the joint.

Move the fence with its stub to the left exactly ½in, and cut another slot to the

▼ *Rout all round leaving a fine cut to finish*

"Whichever jig you use, ensure each of the four box components are symmetrical"

height of the timber workpiece to be used.

With the workpiece held vertically against the fence and butting onto the stub, make your first joint cut.

Move the workpiece to the left so its first slot sits on the stub. Cut the second slot and move the piece to the left again, and so on. Cutting eight combs only takes

a few minutes.

Whichever jig you use, ensure each of the four box components are symmetrical. So, the front panel has comb pins at its base, on both ends; the side panels have cut recesses at their bases on both ends, to accept the pins of the front and back panels.

Cutting list

Birch ply, 12mm thick
2off	Front/back	300 by 100 mm (11³⁄₁₆ by 4in)
2off	Sides	200 by 100mm (7⅞ by 4in)

Birch ply, 6mm thick
2off	Top/bottom	286 by 186mm (11¼ by 7⁵⁄₁₆in)

Dark harewood veneer, (0.6mm thick)
3 leaves	914 by 152mm (36 by 6in)

Dyed veneers leaves for banding, 304 by 100mm (12 by 4in)
2 each	yellow, orange, red
1off	black leaf

Brass piano hinge
1off	276mm by 25mm (10⅞ by ½in)

Leather | Skin gloving leather, minimum 4 sq ft

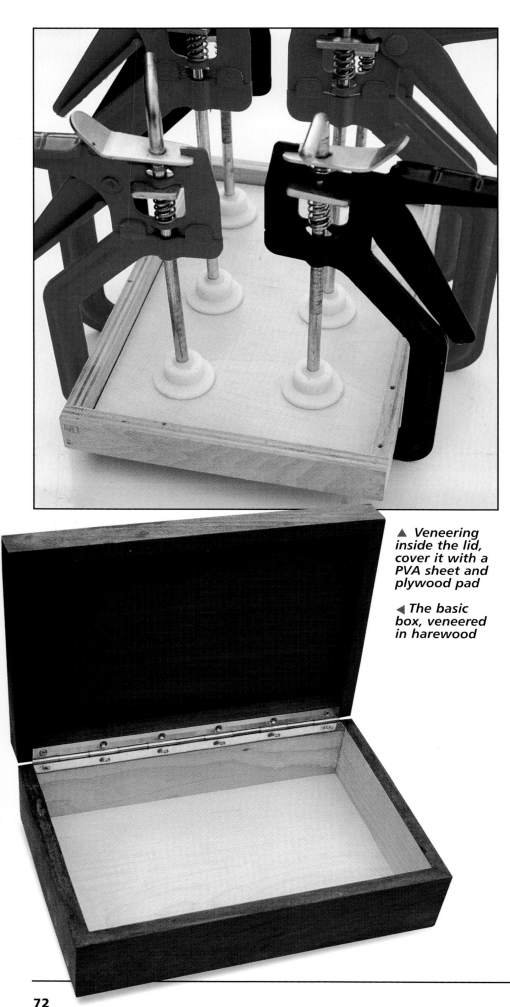

▲ *Veneering inside the lid, cover it with a PVA sheet and plywood pad*

◄ *The basic box, veneered in harewood*

Rebates

Cut rebates along the top and bottom inside edges of all four box pieces. The rebates should be 6mm (¼in) deep and 5mm (3⁄16in) wide, to accept the 6mm (¼in) ply lid/base panels.

Using a ¾in straight cutter and your fine height adjuster, set the cutter to make the rebate in one pass. First test the accuracy of the cut on scrap.

By passing the four box sides completely over the cutter, you will have a very small oblong hole at each corner on assembly. Fill these with plastic wood. It's easier than trying for stopped rebates.

Glue the four combed sides together. Apply white PVA glue to one side of each comb joint and assemble each immediately, as the glue swells the wood.

Check all corners with an engineer's square. If the joint is tight and you need to tap with a hammer, place a piece of scrap timber over the workpiece to avoid bruising the box. Cut the top and bottom panels to fit, and glue them into the rebates.

"First test the accuracy of the cut on scrap"

Lid

When the glue is dry, separate the lid from the box base. I used a ¼in straight cutter for this, in several passes of 2 to 3mm (1⁄16 to ⅛in) at a time. The assembled box is passed over the cutter on its side, and flipped 90° after each pass.

Match the cutter to the 6th joint from the top, so the lid is approximately 31mm (1¼in) thick, and the base 63mm (2½in). The penultimate parting cut should leave about 0.5mm (1⁄32in) of wood all round.

A final pass with the cutter set 1mm (1⁄16in) higher, along the front and back only, will leave the lid joined to the base by only a thin lamination at the two sides. Cut this by hand with a craft saw, and tidy up with abrasive, or plane.

Hinge rebate

The hinge is a length of piano hinge, solid brass, steel pin, cut to match the exact distance between sides, 276mm (10⅞in) on my box.

Place your cut so the end screw holes of the piece are equidistant from both ends.

If necessary, increase the countersunk rims of these holes so the screws you use will be flush or slightly below the hinge surface. Use a countersink bit at low speed, 600rpm.

Measure the knuckle thickness of the hinge when almost closed, but with the sides parallel.

Rebate the back of box and lid to accept this hinge, the depth of each rebate is half the knuckle thickness.

If you are covering the box, allow for the thickness of the covering material of the box rim.

▲ *The box with the colourful dyed veneers chosen for the banding*
▶ *Make the veneers into a block and saw off strips*

"If you are covering the box, allow for the thickness of the covering material of the box rim"

In my case, the hinge was exactly 4mm (³⁄₁₆in) thick. The box base and lid will have veneer 0.6mm (0.020in) thick added later, which must be allowed for. A rebate of 2mm (⁵⁄₆₄in), less 0.6mm (0.020in) means that 1.4mm (¹⁄₁₆in) needed to be cut in each piece.

A fine height adjuster is essential here. I set my ¾in straight cutter to a height of 1.5mm and tested the cut on scrap first.

It was close, with one-eighth of a turn on the fine adjuster. I actually cut two

scraps and checked them together, with two slips of veneer and a piece of the hinge to reproduce the real thing, rather than rely on my ruler. Cut the 1.4mm (¹⁄₁₆in) rebates, up to the inside edges of the box sides.

Veneering
Go slow, paying attention to the sequence of covering, in order to avoid edge grain showing from the front view. It helps to apply front vertical veneers last.

I used a scrap piece of plywood over each piece of veneer, with a piece of plastic sheeting (builder's DPC) between veneer and scrap.

I held this with Solo speed clamps, two each for side panels and up to six for the larger pieces.

For the external pieces of veneer, you can cut oversize, and trim with a scalpel afterwards.

I used white PVA glue slightly diluted – nine parts PVA, one part water – applied to the plywood, not the veneer, which curls when wet.

If you find, when removing the clamps, that the veneer edges are not completely glued, prise the edge of the veneer away slightly with a scalpel, paint diluted PVA into the gap and hold firmly in place with masking tape, after wiping off excess glue with a damp cloth.

"For the external pieces of veneer, you can cut over-size, and trim with a scalpel afterwards"

Banding
This is optional. You can buy ready-made stringings and cross-bandings from your veneer merchant, but these are mostly in brown timbers, not in colours.

I wanted colour to contrast with the sombre grey of the harewood, actually chemically-aged sycamore, available in several shades.

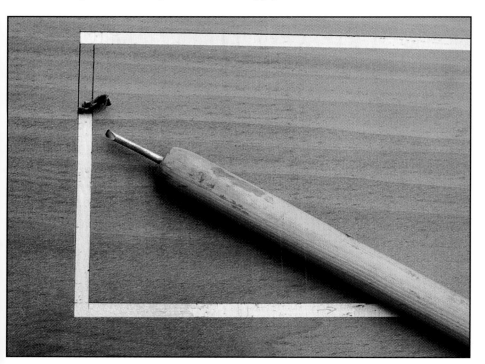

◀ *Remove waste from lid's veneer ready for the banding*

▲ *Pare off the excess thickness of the banding with a sharp chisel*

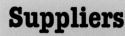

▲ *The nearly completed box with inlay and piano hinge fitted*

I used Italian dyed veneers from The Art Veneer Co. First, make up a sandwich, the cross-section of which will give the banding you want.

There is a choice of 11 colours and black. I used two yellow, and to each side of this core, I added two orange, two red and one black.

Use diluted PVA as before and, when you have added the last layer of veneer, clamp the assembly firmly until dry.

Take the dry sandwiched block, true one long-edge on disc sander or plane, and mark a line about 1mm (¹⁄₁₆in), inside this edge.

Some makers use a bandsaw to cut slices from the block, but I get best results free-hand on my scroll saw.

Inlay

For the top of the lid, mark in pencil an oblong 35mm (1⅜in) in from the box edges. With a colour strip butted up to the inside of these lines, mark the second set

▼ *The last process is to fit the leather lining*

of lines to define the width of the inlay. The inlay on the sides lines up the 35mm (1⅜in) way, and is 6mm (¼in) from the top and bottom.

With a steel rule and scalpel, carefully score these pencil lines right through the veneer. Remove the waste between the parallel cuts. I used a large masonry nail ground to a square chisel end, mounted in a dowel handle, but a carefully set up router with a straight cutter will also do the job.

Cut and fit the oblong inlay, checking the fit exactly – apply diluted PVA glue and hold the pieces with masking tape as you go.

When dry, the excess thickness of the veneer is pared down to the surrounding surface with a fearsomely sharp chisel.

Leather lining

I used gloving leather which is soft, thin and stretches in both directions. I found it impossible to lay a cut section accurately without first mounting the leather onto cardboard formers.

To hide the edges of the leather panels, first cut and glue in, flush with the rim of the box base, strips of wood about 2mm by 8mm (¹⁄₁₆ by ⁵⁄₁₆in), it looks better if the wood tones with the colour of the leather.

Suppliers

Veneers are available from Art Veneers Co, Mildenhall, tel 01638 712550. A leaf of harewood 36 x 6in costs £3.30, dyed veneers 12 x 4in cost 75p each.

Gloving leather is available from ETP Sales & Agencies Ltd, Yeovil, tel 01935 433538.

Top grade leathers about £8 per sq ft, but seconds, like the skin I used, are £1.20 per sq ft.

Routing rectangles

▼Photo 1 *Tidy up your HBs with this attractive box*

Terry Lawrence
continues box-making
with a place to put your pencils

F OLLOWING on from last month's jointed veneered-box project, this time there are no joints to make at all. The base of the box is hollowed from the solid, and the lid is a single plank of timber.

The grooved liner for the pencils is just a piece of MDF. To add a little interest to what could have been a boring oblong, I shaped the exterior to incorporate corner and centre pillars, and inlaid black stringing, again using the router.

You can, of course, include or omit these features, or add your own variations. As before, I used a Trend T5 ¼in collet router, hand-held for the hollowing, and mounted on a Rout-R-Slide table for all other operations.

Tooling up

- ¼in straight cutter
- ½in straight
- 1.5mm straight cutter
- V-groove cutter 90°

◀ **Photo 2** *Cut the perimeter trench, first the long sides...*

▲ **Photo 3** *...then the short ones, note the stops to limit travel*

Box base

If I were making a production run of these boxes, I would prefer to use a proper jig, probably the Trend Pivot–Frame Jig, set up as either an anti-tip frame, or as a ski-frame.

However, for a one-off, I set up the work in the simplest and cheapest way. I clamped the workpiece to the edge of my mobile bench, with pieces of timber of the same thickness fore and aft, so the side fence is kept straight at the beginning and end of the cuts, *see photo 2.*

Pin a strip of timber parallel with the router's travel to the table to support the fence base, keeping the cutter vertical. Pack with cardboard if necessary.

Pin scraps of wood to the front and rear support timbers as stops, this will prevent you over-running.

With this simple set-up, cut the outer groove of the routed interior. Allow 5mm of thickness for the exterior pillars, and 6mm for the wall thickness. This is later trimmed to 5mm. My aim was to create a hollow 193 by 123mm.

Cut a groove in a sequence of passes with a ¼in straight cutter, increasing the depth by 3mm or so at each pass.

For good visibility, I used a spotlight close to the workpiece, but clear of the router, and took the first cut very carefully. I was then able to adjust the two scrapwood stops, with the router stopped.

Approaching the final depth (in my case 29mm, to leave a floor thickness of 5mm), I adjusted the lowest stop on the router to give this depth.

"For good visibility, I used a spotlight close to the work-piece"

Photo 4 *Hollow out the box to the halfway point, then turn it around and finish the other half*

▲ **Photo 5** *Tape the lid to the base and rout the inlay grooves, lid first...*

▶ **Photo 6** *...then the edges*

Rotate the workpiece 180° to do the same gooving on the opposite side of the box without having to move either the end guide blocks or stops.

Rotate the workpiece 90° to continue. I only had to move the nearest end block, as the scrap stop was already set on it.

Waste removal

When completed, there will be an oblong trench all round, 6mm wide and 29mm deep, see photo 3.

The next job is to remove the rest of the waste. I did this with the same 6mm cutter, starting on the right-hand side of the box, taking a 5 to 6mm wide cut from front to rear. Remember to keep the cutter to the right of the timber to be machined.

Deepen the cut by 3 to 4mm at each pass, as before. I used the same depth stop to achieve 29mm on the final pass.

Using the side fence adjuster to move the cutter to the left for the next cut, I found that the standard guide bars were long enough to allow this process to continue to the centre.

At this point the router base plate was supported on the uncut left side, and on the finished side on the right, *see photo 4*.

Rotate the workpiece 180° to complete from the opposite side to the middle, and the box is fully hollowed.

Materials

Oak

1off	Base	215 by 145 by 34mm
1off	Lid	215 by 145 by 10mm

Ebony or black-dyed sycamore

2.5 metres	stringing	1.5mm square

MDF

1off	Pencil tray	230 by 230 by 6mm

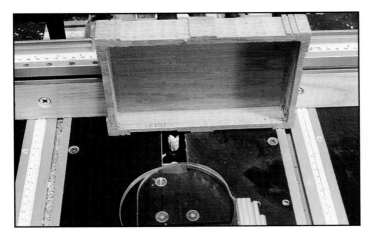

If you need any minor trimming, it can be done now. I cleaned up to give a wall thickness of 5mm.

I used my router at speed No 5, 27,000 rpm, and there were a couple of burn marks inside. These were scraped off with a scalpel, but don't worry if you have any, as they will be hidden by the black interior finish later.

Inlaying the stringing

I used a Wealden 1.5mm cutter for routing the grooves for the 1.5mm square section, black-dyed sycamore stringing,.

Sycamore, being a light hardwood, was left rather hairy from the saw but the thin strips were easily cleaned up with a stroke on each face with a 400-grit sanding block.

▲ *Photo 7 Take the decorative rebate cuts to a depth of 5mm in two passes*

▶ *Photo 8 The box is now ready for the inlays to be inserted*

The grooves in the box can be cut either using stops, or by eye. Mark the positions for the cuts 5mm from the inner verticals of the corner pillars, and then 5mm outside that.

Set the cutter to give a depth of 1.5mm or a little less, but not more, or you would have to sand the oak down to the level of the inlay.

Bring the router toward you and place the lid, upside down, on the table, butting-up to the fence, *see photo 5*.

Align the cutter with the mark, and take the cut, pushing the Rout-R-Slide gently through to the back of the piece.

Move the workpiece and repeat for the second groove, 5mm away. Do this all round the lid, and also on its edges, which are still 10mm thick at this stage.

▼ *Photo 9 A rebate is cut all around the underside of the lid*

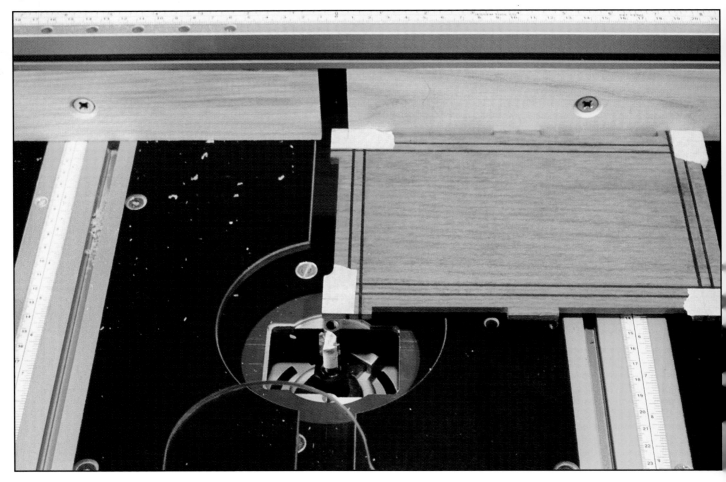

I used a single cut of 1.5mm depth. Two passes would have been better, but I worried that slight inaccuracy might result from the workpiece being hand-held.

The grooves clogged with dust, but the cuts were clean. Next, cut the vertical grooves in the box base to match those of the lid edges, *see photo 6.*

I did not groove the centre pillar, as I felt that carrying these lines over the lid would, by bisecting the top area, detract from the balance of the design.

Inlay the stringing into the 1.5mm grooves, cutting each piece a little overlength. Apply white PVA glue in the groove – not on the stripwood – and press the stringing into the groove with a smooth tool.

I use a miniature spoon-ended tool intended for pewter work, but the small end of a teaspoon will do. Scrape off excess glue.

"The grooves can be cut either using stops, or by eye"

Exterior shaping

First cut the lid from 10mm oak, grain parallel with the long edge. The dimensions must match the base exactly.

Tape the lid to the base with masking tape, then mark the positions of the corner and centre pillars, 25mm in from the ends, and 12.5mm either side of centre.

Between these marks, you need to rebate 5mm. It is preferable just to delineate the areas with a cut first, and then work on lid and base separately.

With the router mounted under your table, and with a ½in straight cutter in the collet, use the fine-height adjuster to set the cut at, say, 2mm.

With a scrap workpiece for practice, adjust the movable stop of the table so the cut matches the mark 25mm in from the left-hand edge. Now place the box/lid package on its edge against the stop and make the first cut.

Do this on all four corners and reverse the work, with lid now facing the rear, and repeat.

You can then remove the stop and take a succession of cuts, moving the workpiece to the left a little each time, until you reach the mark for the centre pillar – these, of course are only on the long sides of the box.

Now separate the lid and box, and deepen the cuts to 5mm all round both pieces, *see photo 7.* If there are any surface inequalities on the vertical surfaces between the pillars, they can be removed with an engineer's flat file, or a cabinet scraper and the box is ready for the inlay, *see photo 8.*

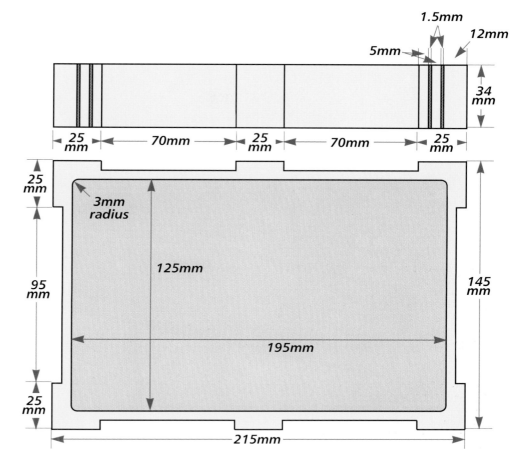

▲ **Fig A Dimensions of the box base**

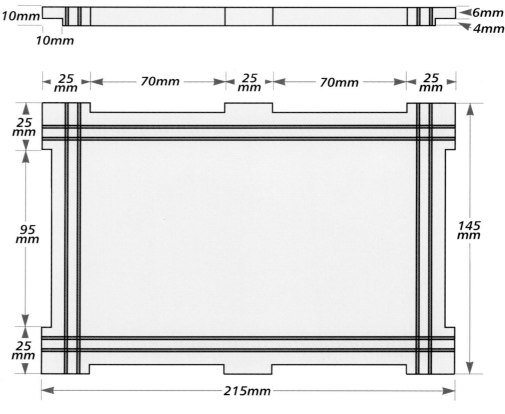

▲ **Fig B Dimensions of the lid**

▲ **Photo 10** *An MDF tray grooved for pencils is stained black*

Lid

It is best to insert the four long pieces of inlay on the lid first. After an hour the glue will be set well enough for you to cut them at the intersections, allowing each of the shorter lengths to be inlaid in one piece, rather than filling in between the first pairs.

With a scalpel, trim off the slight excess at each end, flush with the box surface. Inlay the edge grooves too, and also the matching verticals on the box base.

If the strips are a little proud of the surface, you can either sand or use a cabinet scraper to bring them flush.

Complete the shaping of the lid now, by rebating the under-surface all round, *see photo 9.* You need to rebate 10mm in from the edges, to a vertical depth of 4mm. This can be done in one pass of the ½in cutter, set to the correct depth.

The rebated lid will then match the hollowed inside of the box, except for the rebate's corners, which need to be rounded.

Mark a 3mm radius on these, take a gentle cut with a hand-craft saw. I used a craft knife with a 1in deep blade, 56 tpi. Cut vertically and at 45° to the rebates, and

finish the tiny curves with a scalpel. It's quick, and much easier than setting up the router to do it.

Insert for pencils

To hold the pencils, I made a liner – a flat tray – to fit the routed box. This is just a piece of 6mm thick MDF, with grooves cut parallel and with centres 9mm apart, to a depth of 4mm.

I marked a stick with small vertical lines 9mm apart, and added two horizontal lines, at 2mm and 4mm above the base at one end, representing the depths for the two passes of the V-cutter for each groove.

With the stick at right-angles to the table fence, I could set the position of the cutter for each successive groove, and lock it in that position with the table's cam locking handle.

I found it easier to take two passes for each groove, before moving to the next. It meant fiddling with the fine depth control for each groove, but ensured correct registration.

I cut the MDF to fit the box after grooving, then dyed it with Chestnut black spirit wood stain. The inside of the box was painted black to match, using craft acrylic paint, *see photo 10.*

Finally, the whole box, and lid, were stained with Colron pitch pine stain, which does not affect the black stringing.

When dry, an application of clear Briwax gives a soft lustre to the oak, *see photo 11.*

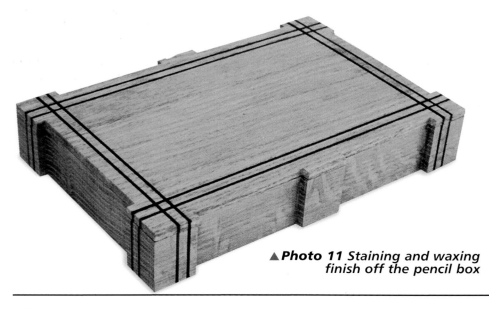

▲**Photo 11** *Staining and waxing finish off the pencil box*

Disc world

Terry Lawrence gets creative and routs a box replica of the island of St. Michel

MOST of you will have seen a photo of the island of St. Michel, which lies on the coast of Brittany, between Avranches and St Malo. The silhouette is like a flattened pyramid, the upper regions fortified with bastion walls, with the Abbey church on top. I loved the shapes, and this 11 compartment box is designed to suggest, not copy, the little island.

The box comprises of three wooden discs, topped by a simplified cruciform church. The slopes of the island are suggested by curved fillets of contrasting wood; the bastions by applied veneer archwork; and the irregularities of the island's volume by steps in alternate quadrants of the base and centre discs.

▲ *Using the Trend pivot frame jig to plane the base disc flat*

Preparing discs

My padauk plank had wind and warp, so I had to flatten the discs cut from it, using the Trend pivot frame jig in ski mode. Photo 1 shows the simple set-up; two battens pinned to the worktop, and a couple

▲ *Routing the interior of the top section using a guidebush*

of pieces of scrap fore and aft of the workpiece.

Fit a 1in straight cutter and a select a speed below maximum, (No. 4, 23,500rpm). With the workpiece between its chocks, convex side uppermost, starting from the right-hand side, push the router over the timber, taking about 0.5mm off the highest point.

▼ *Cutting the top disc*

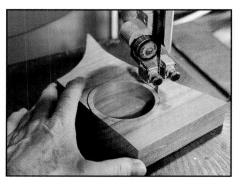

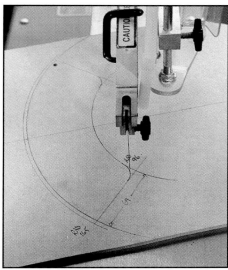

▲ *Cutting the lower quadrants' template on the scroll saw*

Take 1in wide cuts, moving the router on its rods to the left for each pass. This sequence, repeated, should leave the top truly flat. Flip the disc over and repeat for the concave side.

Templates

Screw a 20mm guidebush to the underside of the router base, and set up a ⅜in straight cutter. This assembly is used

▼ *One of the quadrants, routed out to a depth of 10mm. Note outer edge supported by scrap packing*

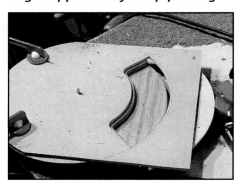

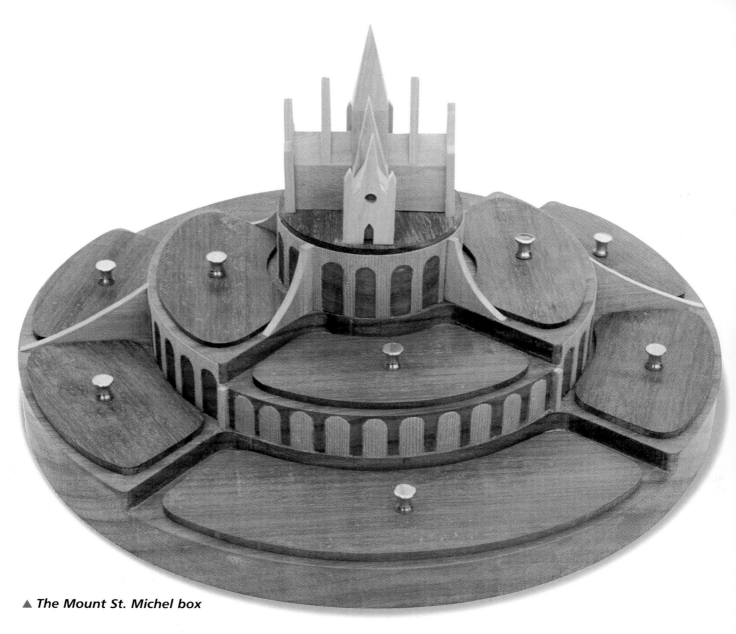

▲ **The Mount St. Michel box**

inside a 6mm thick MDF template, which is clamped to the workpiece, to step the two quadrants of the base and middle

discs, and to rout the box compartments.

To get the correct registration, the templates and discs are drilled centrally to 6mm, the MDF right through, and the discs to a depth of about 20mm. Locate the template accurately with a short length of 6mm steel rod through both.

You will need five templates and, although the diagrams show the

dimensions and curves of the cut-outs in the templates, you may find it easier to lay out each by drawing direct onto the MDF.

The panel sizes may seem rather large, but they will need to be clamped so as to leave the working area clear, and should be supported where they over-reach the workpiece. It's easier to clamp the templates if their blank ends are curved to match the rim of the workpiece below.

▼ **The base, with centre 6mm peg for template registration, and the four small compartments routed**

▲ **The three levels, ready to rout the compartments...**

▲ **...and the three compartments dry mounted**

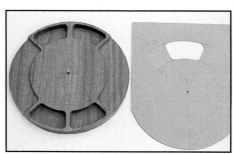

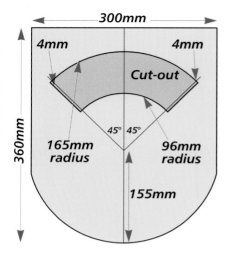

▲ Template 1 *Use to step two quadrants of base disc*

Template 1

On a piece of MDF, 300 by 360mm, mark the centre line, and the centre of the locating peg-hole, 155mm in from one end. With compasses on the peg centre, draw two curves, radii 96mm and 165mm.

Draw two radius lines 45° left and right of the centre line, out to the larger curve already drawn. Draw a line at each end of the curved shape, parallel with the radius line but 4mm outside. This compensates for the difference between the template and the smaller path of the cutter within its guidebush. Now cut out the curved quadrant shape (a No. 5 blade on the scrollsaw is fine), and then drill the peg hole.

This template is used to rout two quadrants of the base disc, 320mm dia, so they are 10mm lower than the other two.

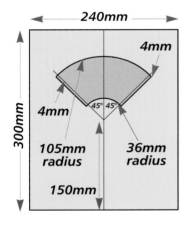

▲ Template 2 *Use to step two quadrants of centre disc*

Template 2

On 240 by 300mm MDF make a pin-hole 150mm from one end. Draw curves at 36mm and 105mm radii. Draw radius lines 45° left and right of the centre line, and again extend the ends 4mm before cutting out. This template is used for routing two quadrants of the middle disc, 200mm dia.

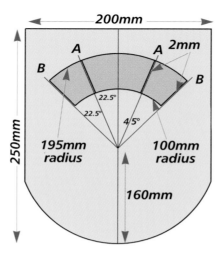

▲ Template 3 *Use AA to rout small compartments in base. Then cut template to BB to rout large compartments in base disc*

Template 3

This is a dual-purpose template, initially cut to rout the four smaller compartments of the base, and then enlarged for the two big compartments. All share the same curvature. On a piece of 300 by 360mm MDF, peg a hole 160mm from one end. Draw curves at 100mm and 159mm radii.

Draw radius lines 22.5° left and right of the centre line, then reduce the template ends by parallel lines 2mm inside the first radius lines. This template is used to cut the four small compartments in the thickest, 30mm, quadrants of the base.

Having routed those compartments, enlarge the template by extending the ends of the curved template cut-out, with radius lines 45° left and right of the centre line. Draw parallel lines 2mm inside these and cut to those inner lines. This template is for the large compartments.

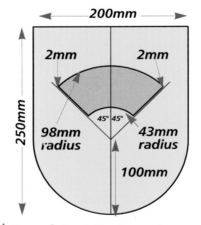

▲ Template 4 *Use to rout compartments in centre disc*

Template 4

On a piece of 200 by 250mm MDF, peg a hole 100mm from one end. Draw curves at 43mm and 98mm radii, with radius lines 45° left and right of centre. Draw parallel lines 2mm inside the radius lines, and cut to these. This template is for the four compartments of the middle, 200mm dia, disc.

▲ Centre disc routed with using template No. 4

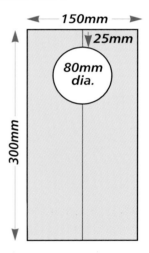

▲ Template 5 *Use to rout top disc and centre of middle disc*

Template 5

Optional, as you could use the scroll saw to cut the top disc. On a 300 by 150mm piece of MDF cut a 80mm dia circular hole, about 25mm from one end of the MDF. There is no need to create a pin-hole.

Use this if you are hollowing the top disc to 70mm internal diameter, which is best done on the remaining piece of plank, before cutting out the disc. This template is also used to rout a central hole in the middle disc, if required.

"Ensure the wood grain of all three components are in the same direction"

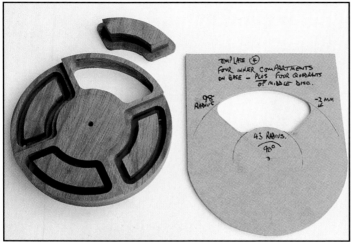

▲ Second disc routed in outline with one of the compartments cut out...

▲ ...and the centre disc finished

Reducing the quadrants

Ensure the wood grain of all three components are in the same direction. On the base disc, 320mm dia, with grain running left to right as you view it, mark north, south, east and west (0°, 90°, 180°, 270°). Bisect these 90° angles and mark lines 45° from each.

Rout the north and south quadrants (315° to 45° and 135° to 225°), reducing their thickness from 30mm to 20mm. Place the 6mm pin in your central hole and lay on template No. 1.

Align its central line with the 0° line you drew first on the timber. Place the assembly at the corner of your bench, centre line at 45° to the bench sides, and the cut-out of the template toward the centre, and clamp.

Use scrap to support the outer end of the template which overlaps the workpiece. If you don't, the router plus your hand pressure will deform the cut, as the MDF will bend at the outer limit of the router's travel.

With a 20mm guidebush and ⅜in straight cutter fitted, set your depth stop to give an initial cut of about 2.5mm to 3mm depth. With the bush located within the template, plunge the router and move it clockwise around the template, then remove the rest of the waste inside this cut.

Repeat, increasing the depth 2.5mm each time until you have removed 10mm, which will leave a thickness of 20mm in which you will rout the large 15mm deep compartments later. Repeat for the second, opposite, quadrant. Follow the same procedure for the middle, 200mm disc, using template No. 2.

Routing the compartments

The procedure is very similar to that for the quadrants. Start with the small base compartments, using template No. 3, supporting the outside of the template with scrap. Remember to locate the template to give equal spacing of the compartments within the thicker quadrants.

It helps if you first draw around the template cut-out onto the wood to see whether you have marked accurately. There should be a 5mm end wall for each finished compartment. Rout each compartment to a depth of 25mm, leaving a 5mm thick floor.

Enlarge template No. 4 as detailed above, and use it for the larger compartments in the stepped quadrants. Routed depth is 15mm to leave a 5mm floor.

When clamping for these larger compartments, ensure that the clamps are over the thicker, 30mm thick, quadrants of the workpiece. If you don't, the clamps will bend the template.

Template No. 4 can be used to rout the middle disc compartments completely but, to avoid much dust and time, I routed only around the outside of the template aperture.

I took this trench to a depth of 25mm, the maximum for safety with my cutter, leaving two thirds of its shank within the collet. I

drilled within this curved slot and cut out the block of waste with the scroll saw.

The surface of the base padauk disc forms the floor of the four middle disc compartments, and the centre circular cut-out. Use template No. 4 to rout four inner compartments in the base, to match the middle disc. This will increase the depth to 55mm. Use template No. 5 to do the same with the centre 70mm dia compartment, increasing its depth to 85mm.

Decoration

Cut four curved fillets from 3mm thick timber (I used Lemonwood), and glue them around the top disc. As you see, they are not at exactly 90° intervals, as I have placed them so that one vertical face is flush with the vertical wall of the routed step quadrant of the centre disc.

Cut and glue two slightly larger fillets, to the wall of the middle disc, each between two small compartments of the base.

Archways

Glue short lengths of veneer strip between the fillets, into which cut archways 10mm wide and 25mm high, at 5mm intervals. The strips are 30mm wide, to match the thickness of the padauk. It is important the grain of the veneer runs across the 30mm width, so it is vertical when glued in place. This ensures it will curve easily to match the curvature of the padauk wall.

Materials

Main timbers	Cameroon padauk (Pterocarpus soyauxii), Lemonwood (Calycophyllum multiflorum)
Arch veneers	Douglas Fir (Pseudotsoga menziesii)
Discs	Padauk 30mm thick, 1 disc 320mm dia, 1 disc 200mm dia, and 1 disc 80mm dia (from a plank 320 by 520 by 32mm)
Lids	Padauk 3 by 3 by 12in (from a strip, 75 by 5mm by 1.4 metres)
Church and fillets	Lemonwood 2 by 2 by 12in
Veneer¨	Leaf or 60 by 300mm minimum
Brass knobs	⅜in, quantity 10
Steel rod	6mm dia, 25mm long
MDF	6mm, 1 sheet, 2 by 4ft for templates

▲ The three discs, fully routed

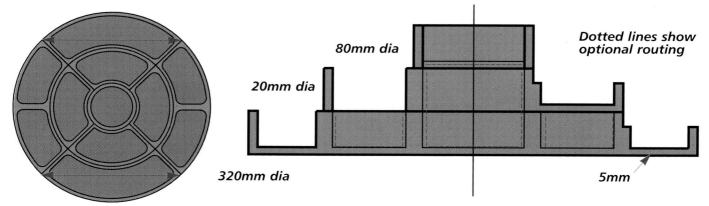

80mm dia

20mm dia

Dotted lines show
optional routing

320mm dia

5mm

▲ 90° quadrant reduced from
30mm thick to 20mm thick

All cutting was done, after marking out in pencil, with a Swann-Mortin scalpel; No. 3 handle and No. 10A blade. Cut each strip a little overlength to produce four complete arches for each top section, and trim to fit.

Use the same pattern for the 30mm thick quadrants of the middle disc, five complete arches for each segment, either side of the lower fillets. The remainder is decorated with the little waste cut-outs from the arch-ways. Reduce their height from 25mm to about 19mm, and glue them on at 5mm intervals. For symmetry, mark the exact layout with a paper strip marked at 5mm and 10mm intervals.

Church

I kept this very simple; a central spire, with four transepts, each with an end facade and a centrally-placed spirelet. All you need is a piece of timber 15mm thick for spire and transepts, and a piece 3mm thick for the rest.

All these pieces can be cut and shaped on the scroll saw, including the transepts which, being only 25mm long, can be placed on their ends on the saw table to cut the roof angles.

A No. 5 blade is fine for the thicker pieces, and a No. 1, at low speed, for the spirelets and pierced facades, pre-drilled with a 0.5mm drill bit. The whole assembly, when glued, is 70 by 70mm, which sits nicely on the lid of the top box.

Lids

Eleven lids are required, all cut from padauk 5mm thick. I cut strips from a square of padauk 3 by 3 by 12in on the bandsaw, at 6mm thick. When planed they finished at 5mm and, being 75mm wide, were large enough for ten lids to be cut from them.

The circular 80mm dia top lid was cut separately from a scrap piece of the plank I originally used for the box discs. The ten curved lids are ⅛in larger all round than the compartments they cover, so, if in doubt, make a paper pattern of the actual routed compartment and check it against your proposed cut on the wood strip. The top circular lid, at 80mm dia, matches the outside diameter of the top disc.

▲ Left: shows cross-section of
two quadrants of full 30mm
thickness for each layer

▲ The Lemonwood fillets added,
veneer rampart arches glued in
place. Waste from the veneer is
used on alternate quadrants

Rebating

Rebate the lids to fit their compartments. I used the router inverted in my router table, with a 1⅜in dia Jesada rebating bit fitted with a 1⅛in guide bearing, to cut a ⅛in rebate. Depth of rebate should be about 2.5mm, half the lid thickness.

Rebate the top lid 5mm to match the thickness of the top box wall. The ⅜in cutter can do this easily. Set its height 2.5mm above the table surface, and position it proud enough of the fence to cut a 5mm rebate.

Bring the two fence cheeks up close to the cutter, and check the cut on scrap first. Push the lid into the cutter until it touches the two

▲ Right: shows cross-section of
two quadrants, stepped at levels
1&2 by 10mm to thickness 20mm

ends of the half-fences, and then rotate. Finally, fit the 10 brass knobs; mine came from The Art Veneers Co, Mildenhall, tel 01638 712550.

Drill each lid centrally to 2.5mm, except the top one which bears the church, and screw in the knobs. Use a scrap of leather in the jaws of your pliers to avoid scratching. Cut off, and file flat any excess screw-tip on the lid underside.

The choice of finish is up to you. I chose a coat of melamine, a light sanding with 400-grit abrasive cloth, and two applications of clear Briwax. Gentle polishing with a soft cloth completes the job.

▲ Rebating the top circular lid 5mm,
(cutter-guard removed for clarity)

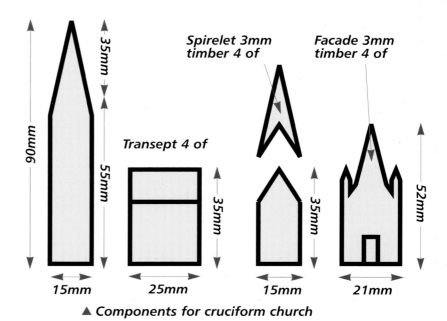

90mm

35mm

55mm

15mm

Transept 4 of

35mm

25mm

Spirelet 3mm
timber 4 of

35mm

15mm

Facade 3mm
timber 4 of

52mm

21mm

▲ Components for cruciform church

Rack attack

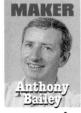

MAKER Anthony Bailey tidies up your music collection with a slot–tastic CD rack

MOST people accept that music CD's give perfect sound, but storing them is another matter. As my collection grew into an unruly pile on the floor I finally gave in and made a revolving CD rack in ash which holds 40 CD's. It takes up a limited amount of room, and looks good anywhere in the home.

The slant of the slots holds the CD's in place and makes for a more dynamic design when filled. This gives a bit of complexity to the design, but here at *The Router* we like a challenge!

Setting out
The key to making this rack is the setting out. You have to know exactly what size the components need to be, and have accurate spacings for the slots.

Start by drawing a side panel showing slots for 10 CD's. Mark even spacings between, plus 5mm extra at each end – this will be the length of the tongue which locates each panel into the top and bottom.

I decided on an 11.5mm slot width to comfortably slide a CD in, and a 9.5mm gap between, with each slot 8mm deep. The slot angle is 35°, resulting in a panel 326mm long by 95mm. Accurately prepare some 20mm thick ash (finished size). All parts must be identical and square.

Slots
Make a jig from 6 to 9mm (¼ to ⅜in) thick ply, with an angled slot towards one end to allow a guidebush to run in. I used a 9.5mm straight cutter with a 17mm guidebush. Any suitable combination will do, providing you make a test slot first to check that you can create the 11.5mm width CD slot needed.

Machine a short angled slot next to

▲ *Keep those unruly CD's tidy in this neat revolving rack*

this, the width of a CD slot and the correct distance from the centre of the guidebush slot. This will give an exact reference position for each successive slot you make.

Screw two strips of wood on the underside so the blanks fit tightly between. Make a test piece first. Position the blank so one end is just in line with the edge of the guidebush slot and cramp in position. This should leave just enough at the end to form the 5mm tongue. Once the first

slot is made, uncramp and slide the blank further underneath so it appears underneath the reference slot in the jig. Reclamp, machine the next slot, and so on.

Side strips should prevent the wood breaking-out at the end of the slots. Create four blanks in this way, then fit the side strips on the other side to create the other four that are a mirror image of the first four. Stick some abrasive on a board to keep it flat and sand all sides and edges of the components to de-fluff them.

▲ *Make the jig for slotting, note the smaller slot to the rear for visually spacing the slots*

▲ *Mark out the jig for creating the housings in the top and bottom panels. The asterisk indicates the datum 90° corner*

▲*Using the plank technique, see panel, to rout the slots*

Top and bottom

Accurately mitre together each of the four pieces needed for the top, bottom and the base. This is quite an undertaking and will show just how good your work and mitre saw is.

A fine-tooth blade, careful setting up, and a test piece are needed to verify that you can get good accurate meetings of all the joints.

The top and bottom can just be butt-glued together, but the base, which is thicker, needs two rows of biscuits for strength, this is because it carries the whole weight of the rack and the CDs. The slots for this are produced with a jointing cutter used in the table.

Tongues

Draw a full-size master drawing or 'rod' of the plan view on a board. I like using white MFC, melamine faced chipboard, the lines are clearly visible and you can use an eraser if you make any mistakes.

Note how the panels sit in pairs offset to each corner, leaving an unfilled space in the middle. This needs a 58mm square piece of ash to complete the equation.

Draw on the 'rod' 6.4mm wide strips aligned to the inside of each panel where their housings will be situated. The tongues on each panel will be flush on the inside slotted face as a result.

Now make a ply jig with slots to take a small guidebush in combination with a 6.4mm straight cutter. The jig will need

two good meeting edges at 90° to each other as it fits flush at the back right-hand corner when clamped on the bottom panel.

The two slots are at the front left-hand of the jig, and there is extra board to the front and side for the router to sit on. The resulting slots on the top and bottom ash panels must match those on the rod exactly, and stop just short of the panel edge so the housed joint is hidden.

Each slot runs slightly beyond the panel at its back end, so the square end of the tongue fits easily into the slot

without having to round the tongue or trimming off. ▶

The plank trick

I have a technique for working on small or awkward-to-cramp workpieces. Screw a long 25mm (1in) or thicker board to the workbench so it projects right out in front. It is then easy to apply cramps along each side and to machine without hindrance.

The deflection of the board caused by plunging the cutter is small, a heavy router will need a thicker board to support it.

Just as pirates of old liked to make their victims 'walk the plank' this is 'routing the plank'.

▶ *The plank technique gives good all round access*

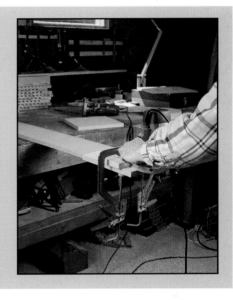

▼ *Again using the plank method, rout the housings in the top and bottom panels*

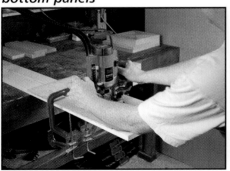

▼ *The jig when flipped over will create the mirror image housings required for top and bottom*

▼ *Rout the tongues on the ends of the slotted panels, machining two together helps to keep them square*

▲ *Nip off the end of the tongues so that the joint doesn't show*

▲ *Use an index stick to position the biscuits slots in the edges ...*

▲ *... and faces to ensure they all line up*

Cut the pieces for the top and bottom panels and the base exactly to their respective sizes, ensuring that the finished corners meet exactly at their mitred junctions in each case.

Using the router and a straight-edge, mark the correct offset for the cutter to edge-of-base distance. Place the jig on the bottom panel and cramp in place so the back right-hand corner and edges line up together.

Rout this and the previous operation by 'routing the plank' as mentioned in the sidebar.

Machine the housings 5.5mm to 6mm deep to leave clearance for the end of the panel's tongues. To cut the housings in the top panel, which is a mirror image of the bottom panel, flip the jig over and mark the critical corner, then rout all four sets of slots as before.

Check that each panel sits in the correct position, flush with the edge of the top and bottom panels and the right width apart to take the CD's cases.

Index stick

All the vertical joints between the panels and the ash 'core' in the middle are made with No.10 biscuits to prevent breakthrough.

Use three per edge and make an index stick with lines 25mm (1in) apart which the cutter must run between to make the slot long enough for the biscuits to fit.

Fit a small block at each end of the index stick so it fits tightly on each blank. Now you can offer each piece up to the cutter in the table and machine the slots exactly, without marking them all individually.

Some joints are on the edges, others are on the unslotted panel faces, so take care in checking which you are doing.

The face slots need each panel to be held vertically as you push it onto the cutter. Always place the furthest end of each panel against the fence first. Don't allow the panel to move backwards over the cutter or it may fly out of your control.

Always swing the panel right away from the cutter once each slot is made so you don't graze the wood between the slots.

The square core piece is 10mm shorter, so adjust the blocks accordingly. All like components will be interchangeable as a result of using the index stick.

Dry fit

Dry fit everything to check that it goes together, then sand all internal surfaces to a finish, taking care not to round over any edges. De-fluff the slots with a folded piece of abrasive paper.

Glue the central panels onto the square core first inserting biscuits and ensuring glue doesn't seep out on the slotted face, if it does wipe it off thoroughly with a damp cloth.

Cramp and check all panels are at 90° to the core piece. Sand the resulting flush surfaces flat. Next glue and biscuit the other panels on and check with a square. Any failure to get this right means the whole thing will not go together when the top and bottom are fitted.

Now glue the top and bottom on, cramp well together and leave to dry.

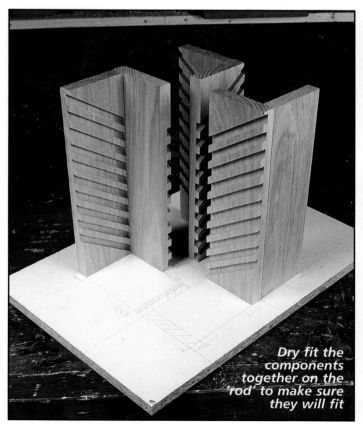

Dry fit the components together on the 'rod' to make sure they will fit

Glue and assemble the main unit together

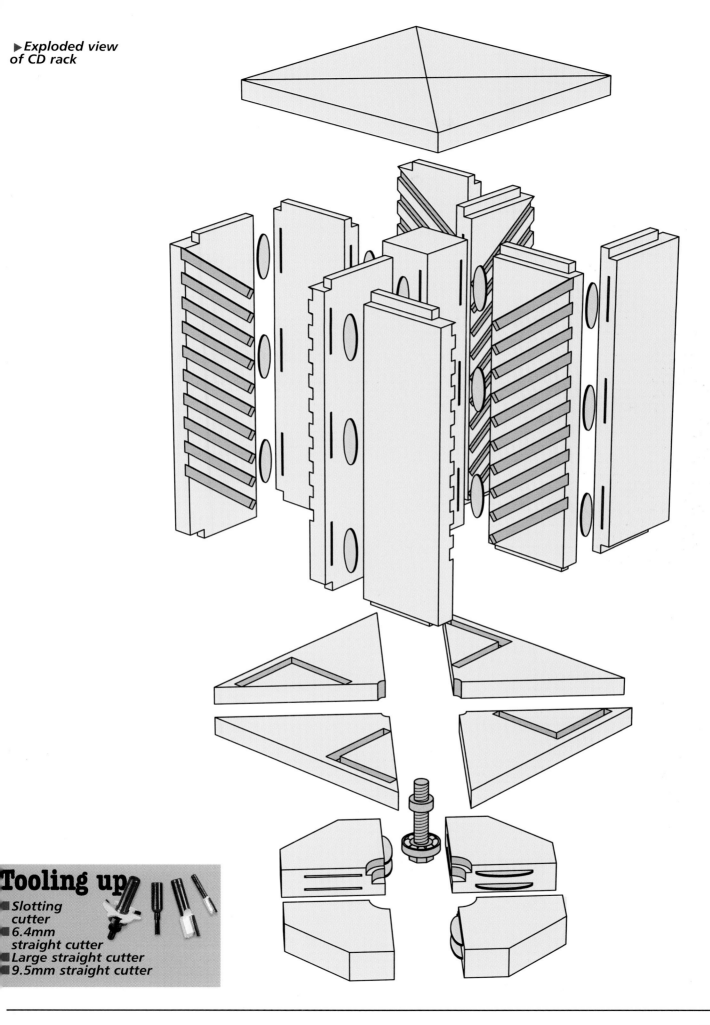

► *Exploded view of CD rack*

Tooling up
- Slotting cutter
- 6.4mm straight cutter
- Large straight cutter
- 9.5mm straight cutter

▲ *Assemble together the bolt and bearing for the swivel, note the housing in the underside of the base*

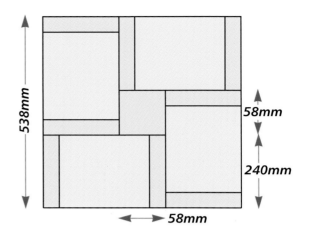

▲ *Apply a finish to the rack to protect it and enhance the grain*

Bolting up

The base must be cut to an octagon, close to the marked lines, then trim with a router and straight-edge. Machine with the grain to avoid tearout.

The CD rack swivels on a large bearing, and a long bolt with nut that fits, in this case a 10mm internal bearing diameter. Draw around the bearing, placed dead centre on the base, take a router and large straight cutter and freehand rout by holding the base.

Work up to the line and check the bearing fit. Adjust by routing until it is a hammer-tight fit. Don't knock it right in or you may not get it out again. If you have a jig passion it would be possible to make one for this process but I decided it would be quicker to rout freehand

Fit the bolt in the bearing and tighten the nut. Now make a further recess underneath so the bolt head will turn freely.

Sand the CD rack to a finish all over, use filler for any flaws or slight gaps, if needed.

Finishing

Upturn the CD rack and mark dead centre. Take a big router with a long 9.5mm cutter, stick some abrasive on the router base so it won't slip around, and make a neat full-depth plunge to drill the bolt hole.

If necessary, trim the bolt to fit the hole and file a bevel on the end to help it start

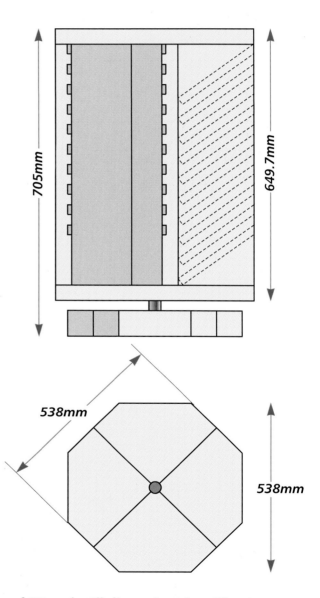

▲ *Dimensions of CD rack. All dimensions in millimetres*

threading, then wind it in with a spanner.

Apply a suitable finish such as sanding sealer or spray lacquer (nothing oily though), tap the base onto the bearing and apply some protective felt or baize. Stand the rack up the right way – it's done!

The last and most vital bit is to fill up the CD rack, pour yourself an alcoholic reviver and unwind after the stress of figuring this project out, listening to the gentle strains of Elgar, Meatloaf or even Fat Boy Slim!

On the case

MAKER

Anthony Bailey

Anthony Bailey
makes a case for
router and cutters

FIND the standard metal cases made for storing routers rather unsympathetic and prefer to make my own wooden ones which are designed to accommodate both cutters and extras. My router is the standard Elu MOF 177E but this case can be adapted to suit any large machine. Take the measurements of the router's unplunged height, width, and depth and adjust the sizes to suit it, leaving space to fit in a fence, fence rods, extraction pipe, guide bush, nuts, spanners, a minimum of 12 cutters on a slide-out board at the top, and collets. If you are working away from your base it is important to carry a selection of cutters to include straight, rebate, ovolo, cove and panel trim, which should cover most types of work.

▲ *A home-made case for your router can be tailor made to fit all accessories as well*

Case

The case is made from 15mm (⅝in) ply with a 6mm (¼in) back panel and a 9mm (⁵⁄₁₆in) door. The cutter board is 15mm (⅝in) thick with stopped holes to prevent the cutters falling through.

In the bottom corner is a slide-out case which contains all the bits and pieces such as guide bush, spanners and small nuts and bolts for fitting accessories. The fence and rods are clipped into the case separately using spring clips and wooden blocks glued to the case interior. The router has a wooden base surround and turn-buttons to hold it securely in place.

The case's jointwork is a good excuse to use the new Trend dovetail jig, the resulting joint giving strength on the corners and looking suitably craftsmanlike at the same time.

Construction

Measure and mark out the case sides, top and bottom. The sides are 9mm (⁵⁄₁₆in) shorter than the overall height as the dovetails are lapped, not exposed.

For both sawing and trimming, I find the Mini-Mach vacuum table very handy – all you need to do is find a flat non-porous surface, place the Mini-Mach on it, attach a

◀ *Set up the dovetail jig for cutting the corners of the case*

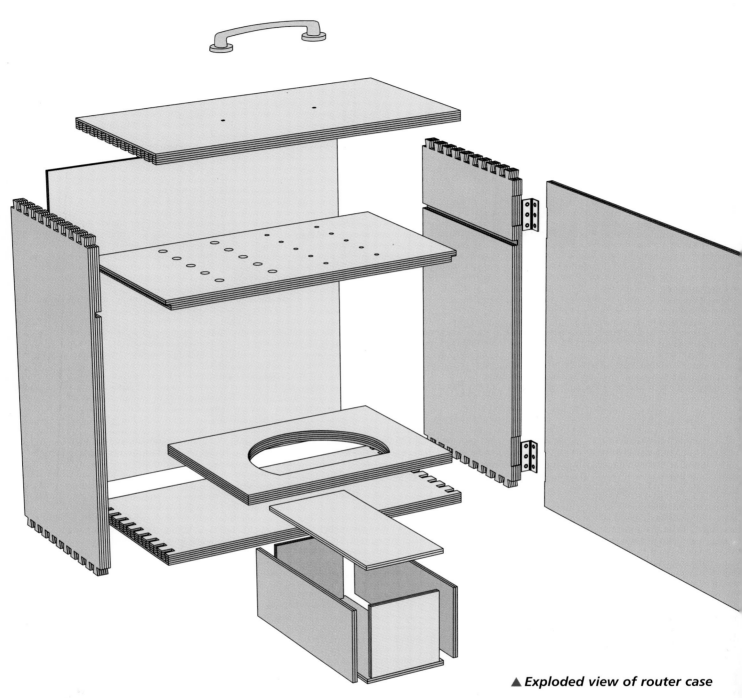

▲ **Exploded view of router case**

domestic size vacuum cleaner to the outlet, and place the board to cut or trim on top, overhanging and ready to machine. Ensure the cutter or blade cannot damage the Mini-Mach and that a reasonable number of 'cells' are covered by the board. If your board isn't quite flat, the foam cell walls will take care of this by squashing down under vacuum pressure – I have sawn ply into strips, lengthwise first, and then cross-cut and trimmed in one go using a router on the MiniMach and a small T-square held in place with spring clamps.

Next, mark the shelf grooves about 95 to 100mm (3¾ to 4in) down from what will be the internal dimension after the dovetails are cut, allowing 10mm (⅜in) for each set of dovetails, and slot about 6 to 7mm (¼in) deep with a 6.4mm straight cutter using the MiniMach and the router's own fence, setting the facings close together for support.

Dovetail jig

Now set up the dovetail jig. This needs to be screwed to a bench edge, or something similar. You could of course use a piece of thick board which can then be vacuum mounted on the Mini-Mach!

"The case's jointwork is a good excuse to use the new Trend dovetail jig, the resulting joint giving strength on the corners and looking suitably craftsmanlike at the same time"

▲ The dovetail joints give the case strength

▲ The back is pinned on then cut to size with a flush trimmer

▼ Before gluing the case together rout the grooves for the sliding cutter shelf

If you are familiar with the Elu jig the principle is the same – set the standard left hand end stop so that when the components are in place, the socket positions will be centred under the template. Each set of stops exactly offsets each of the matching components so that they will line up correctly when assembled.

Cramp the piece to form the socket half of the joint wrong-side up, lying flat on the top of the jig. Now fit the template over it and, holding it down firmly, tighten it up using the knurled brass nuts. The jig should be factory set for making the basic dovetail joint but the manual will explain how to adjust it for different joints.

Having found the correct height setting for the template, insert the vertical component which will have the tails, wrong side showing, and push it tightly up under the template and cramp in place. Now uncramp the socket component and push it tightly against the vertical piece and recramp.

It may sound complex but it isn't in practice! What you have done is to set the jig both in width and in height for cutting an entire set of parts – and the jig remains this way till the job is done. Each time you cut a matched joint, you offer the vertical piece up first. Cramp it, and then butt the flat piece against it, and cramp that too – always wrong side outwards.

Routing

Now take your router and screw the Trend guide bush in place. This fits the jig exactly and has a proper square profile that will run in the jig. Don't use pressed guide bushes that have a rounded internal shoulder.

Fit the dovetail bit – there are alternative cutters available for other joints in conjunction with different templates – and ideally you need a fine depth adjuster, as this allows fine height setting and prevents accidental unplunging.

Sit the router on the right hand end of the jig and adjust the plunge height so that the cutter shows 10mm (⅜in) below the jig. If the router can't plunge low enough you may need to loosen the collet and slip the cutter out slightly.

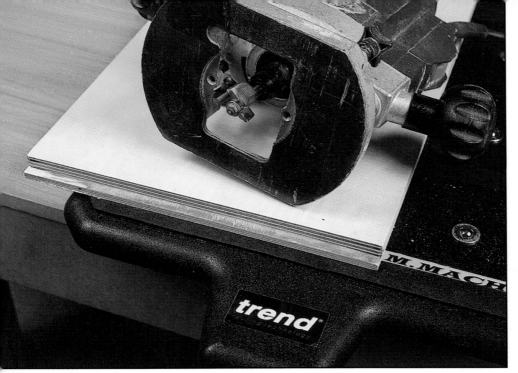

▲ Rout a rebate on both ends of the shelf so it slides in a groove

seem a little aggressive, so keep firm control of the machine at all times. It is worth going back to the beginning and repeating the operation to ensure the tails are properly rounded for a good fit. Remove the router and switch off.

Joints

I found with my test joint that breakout occurred on the wrong face of the tail piece, so to counter this I cramped a piece of scrap 6mm (¼in) ply against the face each time, which dealt with the problem completely. The joint was, if anything, too tight, and since the cutter does both halves of the joint in one hit there seems little you can do to adjust the fit.

When assembling the joints I used a little glue and sash cramps, with wooden pads the full width of each joint, to apply even pressure for neat closure. The result is that

Use scrap pieces for making a test joint – make a habit of sliding the router in from the front of the jig and withdrawing it in the same way which ensures that you need not worry about damaging the work or the jig if the motor is running.

Switch on, push into the first recess and pull out following the shape of the jig, then push into the next recess and so on. Because a dovetail cutter 'undercuts', it can

▼ A jig and guide-bushes will accurately place the holes for the cutter shanks

▲ *With the shelf pulled out, cutters are easy to select*

the joints are tight, neat looking, and incredibly strong.

It is important to remember that the dovetails must be on the side pieces because the weight of the case demands it – if they were at the top and bottom the case could fall apart when lifted.

Inside

Trim the slide-out cutter shelf so it will fit easily in the already formed grooves. The tongue at each end can be made with a small rebater, as the bearing will run along the edge of what will become the tongue – and again this can be done overhanging the edge of the Mini-Mach.

Check the shelf is a loose sliding fit, and make a strip jig for the small router – which makes drilling of shank holes easy. Mine are quite widely spaced but you can set the rows closer to take more cutters if you wish. The standard 17mm guide bush will allow the use of both ¼in and ½in shank cutters, thus giving a mixture of shank holes if needed.

Pin a slightly oversize piece of 6mm (¼in) ply to the back with one edge flush to one side, and then sit the router on the back panel with a bottom bearing guided trimmer fitted, and run round to clean off the excess ply.

Hinges

The case obviously needs hinges, and if they are not the thin pressed type, they will

need to be recessed in. A small router is ideal for this as it will have to sit on the edge, but you should always cramp a thickish piece of wood, say 50mm (2in), along

the side to give extra support. Mark the hinge cutouts with a knife. Plunge the cutter to sit on the case edge, then put the thinnest part of a folded hinge between the depth

▼ *Housings for the brass hinges are cut in with a router*

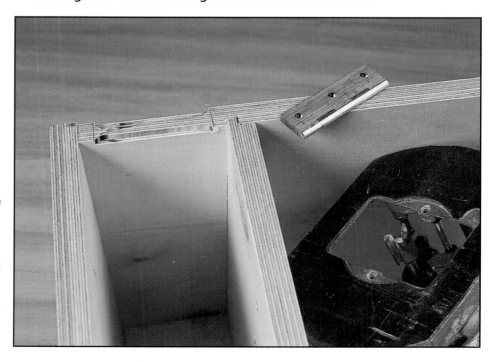

▲ Other accessories can be secured with stick-on Velcro

▲ Turn buttons hold the router securely and spring clips hold the rods

rod and on the capstan stop, and lock the rod. This will give the depth setting – now machine between the knife marks, backfeed the router using a shallow cut in from the side to pre-score the ply. Then, running in the correct cut direction, move in to full width and remove all the ply in the recess area, and try the hinge for fit.

Screw the door in place with the hinge side flush and, as before, trim the other three sides off with a bearing guided trimmer, and then fit the small case catches.

Inside case

In the bottom left hand corner of the case is a box containing all the minor odds and ends – such as nuts, bolts, and guide bushes. The sides can be tongue and grooved if you use solid wood, ply tends to be more fragile when cut open so I glued and pinned my box together. The lid is fixed with stick-on Velcro pieces and this 'cheat' method is also used for holding the dust spout inside the case.

Fitting

The router sits in a hole cut in a piece of ply which fits between the small case and the other case side. Draw the router base shape on the ply,

cut it out and glue in place. Make some pads to glue and screw back and front, on which to fit turn-buttons – each held with a single screw and bevelled on the underside to turn and grip the base easily. The fence and rods are fitted separately using spring clips, and there is plenty of room for other accessories which can be installed with a little ingenuity.

Finish

Tool cases often don't have any kind of finish, but bare wood does get dirty and marked so a couple of coats of varnish are a good idea.

I have fitted a door handle, but if you intend carrying your case around a lot, use a proper case handle which can be obtained from a good ironmongers.

Finally, fit the accessories, cutters, and router into the case!

◀ All latched up and ready to go

Cool carry-case

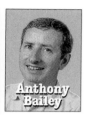

Anthony Bailey takes care of your lightweight routers and cutters with a nifty carry-case

MOST professional routers come with a steel site case, but for some it may only be available as an extra. Small DIY routers don't have cases, though you might find a plastic case at some sort of a DIY warehouse. Steel or plastic, they are rather unlovely things, simply being functional, and not always that.

Casework

For more attractive storage, a properly-fitted box or case is better. I have designed this case to suit a ¼in collet small router, but the design can be modified to accommodate a larger machine.

Note the use of tongue and groove for the casework. This is easy to do, and gives positive location and, once the front and

"The design can be altered for a larger machine"

The completed case with router and accessories

back are on, strength too. There are some internal fittings which are cut to fit the individual machine, and 'turnbutton' strips to hold the router in place.

Also there are Terry clips for the fence and a compartment for all the little odds and ends. I have included a space for keeping half a dozen cutters, on the basis that if you take the router anywhere other than the workshop, you should always have something to cut with, even if you forget the cutter box! A large case handle is needed, which are available from hardware shops, and the hinges need to be recessed in.

Getting started

First of all cut some strips of 12 by 140mm wide ply, long enough to get all the case parts out of, except for the door and the back which we will do later.

Casework tongue and groove

Note the sliding cutter board and turnbutton strips`

Materials

Two case sides	410 x 140 x 12
Top and bottom	360 x 140 x 12
Left-hand vertical divider	232 x 140 x 12
Base and shelf piece	140 x 90 x 12
Slide-out cutter board	139 x 89 x 12
Right-hand vertical divider	210 x 140 x 12
Divider front piece	120 x 50 x 12
Shaped piece to hold router base (2)	140 x 110 x 12
Case door	410 x 360 x 9
Back panel	410 x 360 x 6
Two short wood strips to make turnbuttons	60 x 30 x 10

16mm fixing pins for back panel
PVA glue
Four small Terry clips
Pop rivets
Short screws
Hasp, staple, and padlock
Flip-down brass handle
Formica for under slide cutter board, and contact adhesive
Two small brass hinges

*The completed case
with flip-down handle,
hasp and staple with padlock*

Cut all the pieces to length and check you have the correct number and sizes of components. Since most components are housed together using a tongue and groove this is included in the component sizes, some having a tongue at each end, others one end only.

Grooves

Machine the grooves first, using a 6.4mm straight cutter on the router table and a mitre protractor or a good square pushblock. You could do this freehand using a fence, though care is needed for a decent result.

Now machine the tongues using a larger diameter straight cutter again on the table and aim for a good tight fit. For all these operations fitting a through-fence will help the components slide across the fence opening smoothly.

Assemble all the components using PVA glue and 1½in panel pins, clean up, check for square and leave to set.

Now cut out a piece of 6mm or thinner ply for the back. This should be a fraction oversize. Glue and pin in place and use a small router and a bearing-guided cutter to trim exactly to case size.

Note that the pins must be flush with the surface or they will scratch the router base. Use a straight cutter or shallow mortice cutter if you have it, to achieve the neatest results on the hinge recesses.

Place the thickest part of the unfolded hinge under the depth stop rod after bringing the cutter down to surface level. Lower the rod to trap the hinge, this should be the correct recess depth.

Mark the hinge positions on the carcass and do the recesses with a strip of wood clamped alongside for extra router support.

Cut a piece of board slightly oversize again, as the door. Mark the hinge positions and recess as before. Screw the hinges on and close the door then trim the three unhinged edges as you previously did with the back panel.

*The back of the case.
Note the pop rivets
used to fix the Terry
clips inside*

Handle

The handle needs to be bolted on if possible and the various clips fitted in place using long pop rivets and a drill to make the holes for them.

The cutter board should be a slightly loose fit and has two rows of holes drilled using a 6.4mm straight cutter in the router aiming on to cross lines wherever the holes need to be.

Use a larger piece of board and cut to size, that way the router will sit easily on it. The result is more precise than an ordinary drill so long as the router does not slide around whilst drilling; a good tip is to stick abrasive paper on the router base to prevent this kind of slipage.

Finally a hasp and staple with padlock complete this project and possibly a coat of varnish. Now your precious machine can sit tidily and safely on a shelf until you need it and it can also be carried about.

Tooling up

- Pop rivet gun
- ⅛in straight cutter
- ¾in straight cutter
- Bearing guided cutter
- T-square

Crafty cutter container

Bill Cain makes a lidded cutter box the easy way

K EEPING router cutters in good condition isn't always too easy, their seemingly tough tungsten edges are easily damaged if a couple of them clash into each other, when stored loose in a drawer for example.

Most cutters these days are supplied in individual storage cases – some are more sturdy than others. This is all very well, but each case takes up quite a lot of room and if a large number of cutters are owned you seem to obtain a disproportionate amount of plastic.

Themed cutter sets are often supplied in a sturdy wooden box and this is where the inspiration for this project came. They keep all cutters safe, dry and neatly in one handy to carry storage unit.

There is nothing too challenging about this project. A box is after all just a box, so vary its size to suit your own needs and allow some space for a growing collection.

Regardless of the size, I find such boxes always become too small as the number and sizes of cutters in a collection grows, so I made quite a deep box as some cutters can be around 100mm (4in) in overall length.

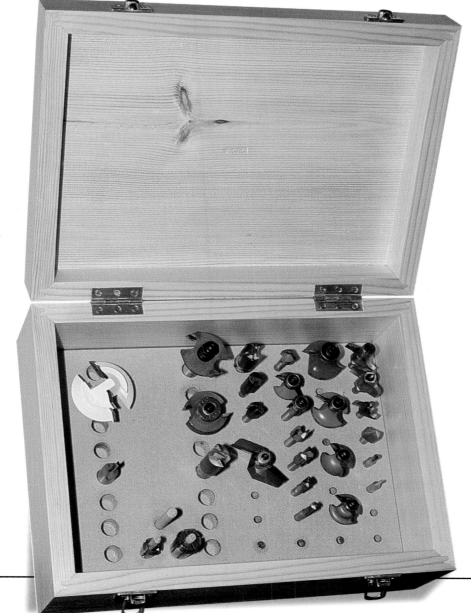

◀ A well made storage box keeps your cutters in good condition

▲ A typical container that a cutter is delivered in, the one shown houses the cutter used to make the box

▲ Rout the lock mitres on the ends of the long ...

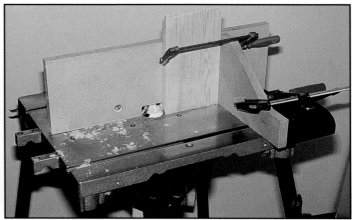

▲ ... and short box sides

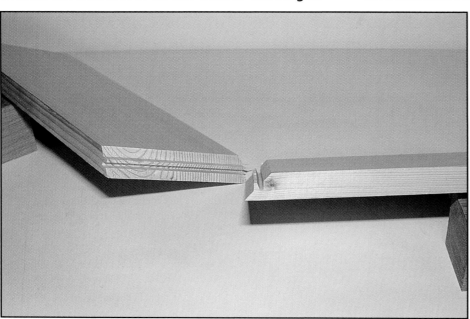

▲ The lock mitre joint ready for assembly

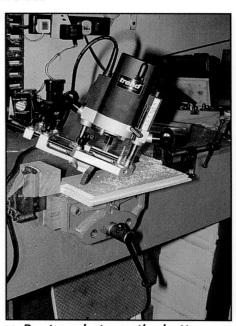

▲ Rout a rebate on the bottom inside edge for the box's bottom

▼ Part the lid from the base with a small diameter cutter

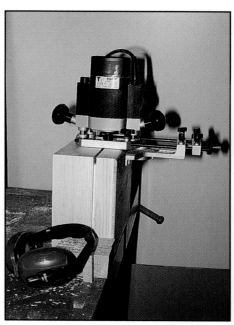

"Regardless of the size, I find such boxes always become too small"

Suitable materials for cutter boxes are 17mm (⅝in) thick softwood with a 6mm (¼in) ply or MDF bottom. This should be plenty strong enough, but a hardwood such as beech would probably be better. Its added durability is preferable for the larger box, as its surprising how heavy a set of cutters are when together in one box.

Tooling up

Routers
- Trend T5E
- Elu 117E/table

TCT Cutters
- Jesada 'Junior' Lock Mitre supplied by APTC
- APTC ¼in and ½in diameter straight 2-flute
- APTC 9.5mm radius rounding/ovolo

Sides

Prepare and thickness the stock for the sides and top, plus some extra pieces for experimenting with the router's settings, especially when using the lock mitre cutter which can be tricky to get accurate results.

Cut the sides to length and trim the ends square ready to be jointed. Rout the lock mitre joints on the ends of all the components – this cutter must be used in a router table. It is important to find the cutter's centre point, when setting its height and the table's fence, which is crucial to a good fitting joint. Once set, timber can be run past the cutter, orientated either vertically or horizontally to create an 180° joint for edge jointing or a 90° joint for corners.

Next, rout a 6mm (¼in) deep rebate into the bottom interior of the sides to take the bottom panel.

Sand and finish the interior faces of the sides; this job is always easier before assembly while the parts are flat.

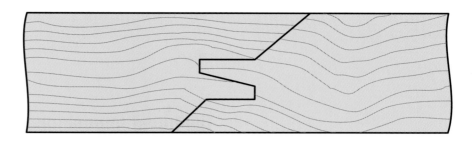

Glue the sides together and ensure they are held square while the glue dries, then cut the bottom panel to size and fix it in place with glue and screws. It is easier to finish the interior before assembling.

Lid

Run a lock mitre joint down the length of two boards, this is the 180° method, to create a board wide enough to make the top of the lid. Leave the pieces oversize on length to allow them to be accurately cut to size when made up in one piece. Glue the pieces together, then sand and finish the face which will become the interior of the top.

Next, rebate the interior face of the top, making it partially inset to form the lid. Glue the top into the box and run a roundover moulding around the top to soften the edge.

You now have a totally enclosed container without any method of getting anything into it, and the reason for making the box

▲ *The lock mitre joint is useful to edge join the boards that make up the box lid*

this way is because making a lidded cutter box in separate parts seems to me to be hard work as there is the obvious potential for size variations between the lid and the box.

Separating

To separate, I used a small 6mm (¼in) diameter straight cutter fitted into a Trend T5E. With the side fence in place and the box secured firmly to stop it moving around, I ran a cut all around the box in three increasing depths until the lid was separated from the box.

To finish, sand all the faces and install hinges or catches, making sure that the lid

is fitted the right way round. This may sound obvious but it will be distressing if all the hard work that went into making it an exact fit was blown at this stage.

The interior storage will need to be tailored to your own cutter collection. I cut and drilled the cutter holding plate from MDF, leaving it as a loose fit into the bottom of the box.

As I have a selection of ¼in, 8mm and ½in shank cutters, I planned the holes for them so they were arranged neatly into easy to find groups. Drill the holes for the cutter shanks with a little clearance so the cutters are easy to take in and out, if they are stiff there is a danger of cutting your fingers.

▼ *Dimensions of my cutter box*

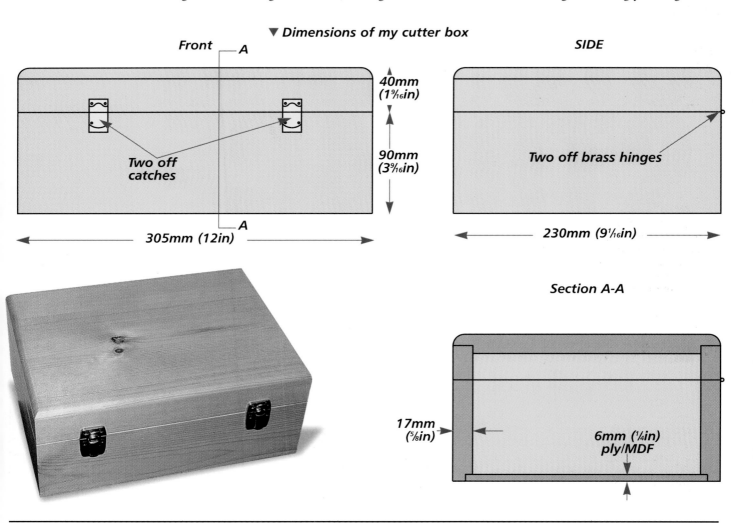

Front — A

40mm (1⁹⁄₁₆in)

90mm (3⁹⁄₁₆in)

Two off catches

A

305mm (12in)

SIDE

Two off brass hinges

230mm (9¹⁄₁₆in)

Section A-A

17mm (⁵⁄₈in)

6mm (¼in) ply/MDF

Richard Stevenson suggests that shelves in the workshop may be the best way of tackling the all too common problem of lack of storage space

STUNNING STORAGE

L ike most other workshops, mine is in a constant state of evolution as the passage of time, or acquisition of tools and/or equipment makes changes to the current arrangements necessary.

When I moved four years ago to this rural area in the West Country, I was completing a City and Guilds course in furniture-making with a view to setting up my own business. Although none of the original farm buildings remained, I was lucky enough to have a suitable space for construction of a workshop of about 9 x 5m just across the yard from the house.

On completion, I moved in the various old and new machines I had acquired with all the rest of the paraphernalia of benches, tools, clamps, sharpening equipment etc. and marvelled at the luxury of it all. Apart from my workbench, my table and storage arrangements consisted of various bits of MDF, chipboard and plywood, supported on piles of concrete blocks and bricks, a short section of Spur shelving on one wall, and lots of plastic storage boxes. While this was all a bit rough and ready, overall the arrangements were very functional, and survived for a year or so, enabling me to get a few jobs under my belt.

LET THE GAMES BEGIN

Eventually though I decided that improvements were necessary to clear up the floor space and make things easier to find. I didn't want to spend a lot of time and money on making elaborate cupboards so I bought several sheets of construction grade 18mm (23/32in) plywood and set to work with a saw, hammer and a few nails. Along two of the walls I built a worktop 600mm (24in) deep, with the space below divided into compartments about 600mm (24in) wide with a fixed shelf at half height. These compartments

are ideal for keeping power tools, containers of glue, finishing materials etc. and their dimensions allow for the use of the ubiquitous plastic storage boxes - the next best thing to a chest of drawers, (**see photo 1**).

On the window side worktop I placed my drawing board and sharpening equipment, to take advantage of the natural light, and on the other I built a shelf unit 300mm (12in) deep and from worktop height to 2400mm (96in). I again spaced the uprights at 600mm (24in) to match the compartments below, and drilled a vertical series of 8mm (5/16in)

holes, inset from front and back, through each upright to provide an adjustable shelving arrangement. The shelf supports are pieces of 8mm (5/16in) dowel located in the holes at the required height, which fit into recesses drilled into the bottom of each shelf with a 10mm (3/8in) Forstner bit, (**see photo 2**).

To drill the vertically spaced holes, a simple drilling guide is required. The accuracy regarding the spacing of the holes is not so critical, but for the shelves to sit properly on their supporting pegs, the holes must be at exactly the same height at each side of the shelf. The eas-

iest method of ensuring this is to make a template from a length of 18mm (23/32in) MDF the same width as the shelves, drilled with two sets of 8mm (5/16in) holes at the chosen spacing. This is used as a guide to locate the drill for all the shelf sides so that even if not quite accurately spaced, the supporting pegs at both sides of the shelves will be the same height. The chances of achieving this by separately marking out and drilling each piece are probably similar to the lottery odds.

Although in theory the shelves are identical and should fit anywhere, in

Photo 1 Plastic storage boxes are a cheap and quick solution

Photo 2 Ply is tough and hard-wearing. Note the use of wedges to level unit

Photo 3 Each chisel is stored separately

Photo 4 The thick door framing allows a lot of storage

"It is preferable to use hardwood here, as softwood runners don't have a long life expectancy."

practice, due to the somewhat crude method of the construction of the frames, the sections of shelving are not quite consistent in width, which results in a limited interchangeability. This is a small price to pay for the speed of construction. Nailed together components may seem flimsy to those used to using dovetails for carcass construction, but the main shelf supporting sections are fixed to the wall as well. The final edifice is solid as a rock.

A JOB WELL DONE?

So after a couple of days work I had a storage system that I thought fulfiled all my requirements. The workshop seemed

even larger with everything in its place, and as I could easily find the tool I needed, efficiency was improved.

Of course, working with any arrangement you begin to find its weaknesses and ways of refining the system come to mind. After about another year, I decided that storage of tools on open shelves was probably not the best method. No matter how good your dust extraction system is, a workshop is a very dusty environment and I was tired of having to brush the dust off every tool before using it.

Some form of enclosure was obviously needed, so I decided to fit 12 large but shallow drawers into the compartments

of the base section below my shelf unit. Not having a dovetail jig for my router, and wanting a speedy solution to the construction, I nevertheless felt that something more sophisticated than a hammer and nails was called for if the drawers were to function successfully.

PLAN B

I made the front, back, and sides of each drawer from 12mm ($^{15}/_{32}$in) parana pine plywood as construction grade ply, is very rough. The fronts and backs were rebated at each end on my shaper (similar in operation to a router table). A

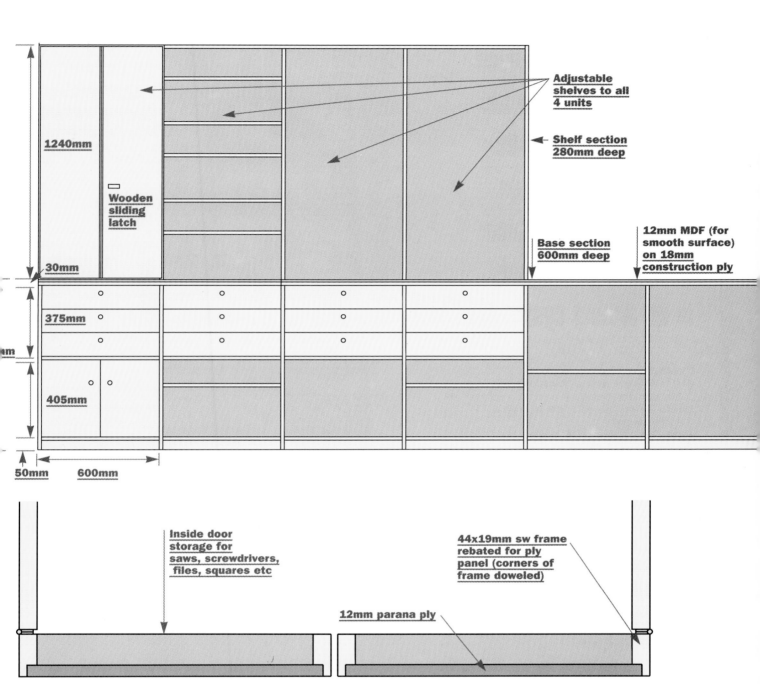

1240mm

Wooden sliding latch

30mm

375mm

405mm

50mm **600mm**

Adjustable shelves to all 4 units

Shelf section 280mm deep

Base section 600mm deep

12mm MDF (for smooth surface) on 18mm construction ply

Inside door storage for saws, screwdrivers, files, squares etc

44x19mm sw frame rebated for ply panel (corners of frame doweled)

12mm parana ply

groove to take a 6.35mm (¹/₄in) MDF base was formed in the front and sides using the same machine, and the whole assembly glued and pinned together. Using ply construction with an MDF base means, of course, that no movement has to be allowed for, so the bottom can be glued in all round, and this results in a surprisingly strong drawer, even though each one measures about 600 x 600mm, (24 x 24in).

The drawers run on 20x10mm (²⁵/₃₂ x ³/₈in) strips of oak or maple from the off-cut bin, screwed to the sides of the car-cass. It is preferable to use hardwood here, as softwood runners don't have a

long life expectancy. To accommodate the runners, the depth of each side of the drawer is reduced by 22mm, (⁷/₈in) and when the drawer is inserted, the runner of each also acts as the kicker for the drawer below, preventing sagging when opening. In fact the runner is also the stop for the drawer below. When fixing the runners I made them too long by a few mm and shaved them back with a chisel to allow each drawer to enter to the same point.

I made a similar drawer under my sharpening station to take various jigs for the Tormek grinder, along with honing guides and bits and pieces, and two

smaller ones beside my drawing board for pens, pencils and scales etc. I now found that I had an embarrassing amount of drawer space, and some of it is under-used. This is still preferable to not enough as things tend to accumulate over time.

My chisels are kept in simple sliding racks in two of the drawers – a sheet of 6.35mm (¹/₄in) MDF with strips of maple Superglued on as divisions. The rack is tilted up at the back by tapered strips glued underneath. These slide on hard-wood runners so the top rack can be slid back to give access to the rack below, (**see photo 3**).

"...and I had achieved all I had set out to do — at least until I discover the inevitable shortcomings, which seems to be roughly in an annual cycle..."

Photo 5 Everything in its place
Photo 6 Every surface holds tools with plenty of room to spare
Photo 7 Note this natty use of dowels for shelf support
Photo 8 Cosy storage for planes. Note the unusual door locking handles

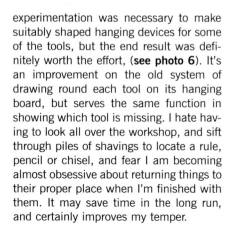

Power tools do not easily fit into drawers, so to alleviate the dust problem I fitted in doors, again of 12mm (15/32in) parana ply to the front of their compartment. Door and drawer pulls are simply 30mm (11/8in) holes, which although allowing a little dust penetration are cheap and cheerful, (**see photo 4**).

To store the rest of my hand tools I fitted a pair of full height doors to the front of one section of my shelf unit. More 9mm (11/32in) parana ply on a simple rebated and doweled softwood frame provides doors of a depth suitable for hanging saws, screwdrivers, spokeshaves, squares and rules, (**see photo 5**). Some

experimentation was necessary to make suitably shaped hanging devices for some of the tools, but the end result was definitely worth the effort, (**see photo 6**). It's an improvement on the old system of drawing round each tool on its hanging board, but serves the same function in showing which tool is missing. I hate having to look all over the workshop, and sift through piles of shavings to locate a rule, pencil or chisel, and fear I am becoming almost obsessive about returning things to their proper place when I'm finished with them. It may save time in the long run, and certainly improves my temper.

Planes, scrapers and other items are

housed on the now enclosed and dust free shelves, with the planes sitting on thin strips of wood under the toe to protect their edges, (**see photo 7**). A little playtime produced a maple sliding latch and locking bolt to hold the doors closed. Not the quickest solution maybe, but fun nonetheless, (**see photo 8**).

All that remained to be done was to make a door to keep dust off that other vital piece of workshop equipment, the stereo, and I had achieved all I had set out to do — at least until I discover the inevitable shortcomings, which seems to be roughly in an annual cycle, and the next development takes shape.

Stone store

MAKER
Anthony Bailey

Anthony Bailey routs a protective box to keep his oilstone out of trouble

▲ *A box for your oilstone will keep it in good condition*
▼ *Cut the two long parallel slots in the jig*

O NE of the most useful basic workshop items is a good oilstone, because we still need all the basic handtools despite the onslaught of routers and other powertools.

Planes and chisels need regular sharpening and frequently don't get it! I own two stones, one is standard coarse and medium grit, the other a much finer stone which definitely deserves a box, especially as it picks up dust and chippings and leaves oily abrasive particles wherever put down.

Measuring up

Measure your oilstone and make a jig for use with a router and guidebush that will create recesses in the base and lid of the box. Most stones are now standard metric sizes, in my case this was 200mm x 50mm x 25mm (8 x 2 x 1 in).

Use a piece of thin ply or MDF for the jig, measure the difference between the cutter and the guidebush, divide the result and you get the amount by which the jig aperture needs to be over and above the size of the stone.

Allow a fraction more so the stone will actually fit, but not enough for it to slip around.

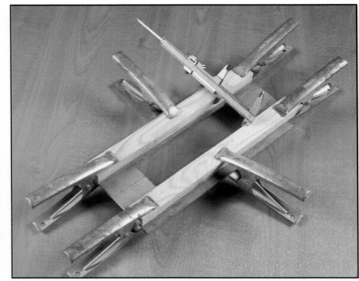

▲ *Set-up for the end cuts that will complete the cut out* ▲ *Fix on the runners that will position the jig*

"Beech is commonly used, but I have a penchant for good quality ply"

Tooling up

■ **Straight cutter**
■ **Bearing guided 45° cutter**

Slotting

Set up the router table with the fence loosened at one end so you can drop the ply onto the cutter well within what will be the waste area. Move the fence forward and lock it once the cutter is touching the marked line.

Hold the ply carefully against the fence and move up to the cross lines at each end so you have a neat slot. Switch off, lift the ply and turn it, then repeat the operation, ensuring you end up with parallel slots the correct overall distance apart.

Fit the mitre fence, or use a square piece of board, and machine the end slots. It is important to support the right-hand end, as the cutting action can cause drag, and you will end up with a slightly uneven slot.

Repeat at the other end, taking care as the waste piece comes away. If necessary use a file to tidy the aperture.

Saw and glue two strips of softwood either side of the aperture, leaving a centralised parallel gap between to take the width of the box (mine was 70mm). Cramp, clean off excess glue and leave to dry.

"Allow a fraction more so the stone will actually fit, but not enough for it to slip around"

▼ *Carefully rout the recess in the ply*

▼ *Slide the jig along and rout the second recess, make sure there is enough space between the two recesses*

▲ Fit the two pieces onto the oilstone and while it holds them together cut the box to length
▼ Rout the finger grips using lines marked on the box and sub-fence to position the cut

▲ Rout a small chamfer all around the top and bottom of the box

Jigging

Choose your box material. Beech is commonly used, but I have a penchant for good quality ply, especially if it has an interesting colour with a finish applied.

Cut and plane to width a strip long enough to do at least one box, though you may want to make up several more if you own other stones, but bear in mind they may be different sizes.

The wall thickness is slightly greater at the ends because of the 'short grain'. By having a jig that straddles the wood you can slide it along and make as many parts as there is wood for.

Cramp or pin the jig so it can't slip, sit the router on and adjust the depth setting for a 13mm deep cut. Use the depth turret for machining in three passes to depth.

Move the jig along and repeat. The distance between isn't critical, so long as the recesses aren't too close.

Guidebushes are often deeper than the 6mm ply I favour, so I ground one down so it doesn't protrude below the ply.

Tight fit

Square the recess corners with a chisel, if you don't fully square the corners on the bottom box-half it will hold the stone nice and tight, while the top half will lift off easily. Fit the two pieces around the stone, check it fits and closes, then mark one piece where the box ends' should be.

◄ Drive panel pins into the underside, leaving the points exposed so they grip the bench and hold the stone secure while in use

Dimensions of oilstone box

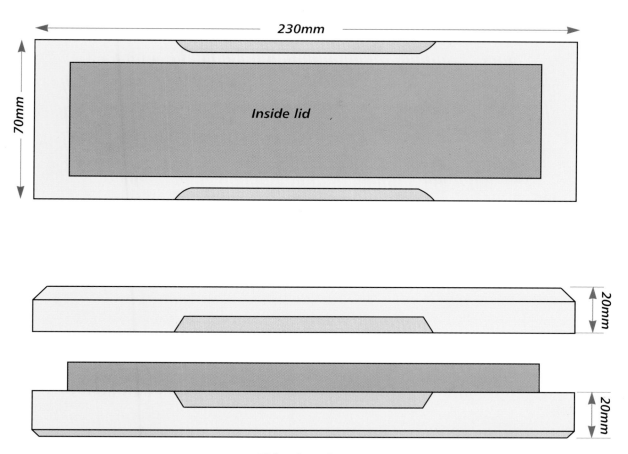

230mm

70mm

Inside lid

20mm

20mm

Side elevation

Crosscut the 'sandwich' on your marks to give neat matching ends – don't accidentally cut through where the stone is! Apply all faces to the belt sander, with the stone still locking it together.

Chamfer

Remove the oilstone and set up a chamfer cutter in the table to create the finger grip. Fit a sub-fence and make a test cut on a waste piece of ply. Switch off and mark the ends of the chamfer on your test piece, then turn the cutter till it just rubs against one end of the stopped chamfer.

Transfer the mark onto the sub-fence and repeat at the other end. Mark each side of the box lid where you want the chamfer to start and stop, transfer these marks across both the top and bottom halves, and use the sub-fence marks as your guide points for starting and stopping.

Apply the wood on the far end-mark first to avoid a kickback. Move it smoothly along and slide the tail end away when you reach the second mark.

Don't linger during the cut as it will burn. Reset the cutter a fraction higher and pass again to remove any burns.

It is possible to fit start and stop blocks on the sub-fence. These are more positive if you are making several boxes.

Finishing off

The last operation is to machine the lid top edge all round with the same chamfer cutter, though at a lesser depth, then make a small chamfer on the base as well.

▼ **The finished item ready for use**

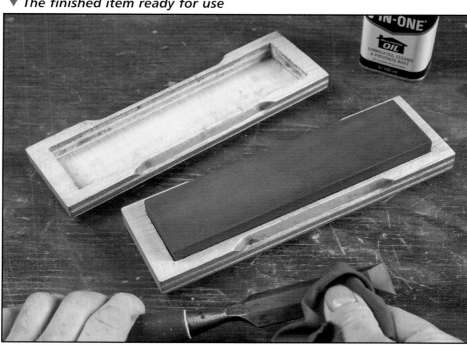

Fine sand all faces and apply a varnish on the outside. For the final touch, pre-drill and fit panel pins so the points just protrude underneath, holding the box firmly on the bench-top when sharpening.

OTT with oysters

MAKER

Ian Hall

Ian Hall sees no reason why an engineer's tool-box cannot be beautiful as well as strong

H AVING worked as an engineer on the shop floor of an aircraft facto-ry for 30-odd years now, and also being a keen amateur woodwork-er, I realised recently that I had never got around to making the traditional wooden engineer's toolchest that I had yearned for since I was an apprentice.

I was also driven to the drawing board by the browbeatings of a friend who wanted one, and by the fact that I have a veritable moun-tain of offcuts in various woods and all under 610mm (2ft) long.

I was further spurred on by a retiring shift-mate, who pointed to my metal cantilever-style box and told me it was of the type used only by mechanics. Ouch! And my apologies to readers in the garage business.

I ended up making three toolboxes, in laburnum (*Laburnum anagyroides*), pear (*Pyrus communis*) and mahogany (*Swietenia macrophylla*). The drawer sides are mainly oak (*Quercus robur*), their backs are laurel (*Terminalia sp*) and a little plum (*Prunus sp*) crept in here and there. Apart from the oak and mahogany, which are reclaimed, the rest of the timber is from local garden clearance.

Door front

The fronts ended up rather ornate and are superfluous. At the design stage they started as conventional frame-and-panel style, that is until I realised, as the job progressed, that there was not enough laburnum to make a solid panel. I did, however, have a smallish well-figured chunk with which to

▼ *An engineer's chest beautifully made to fulfill a lifelong dream*

"The locating tongue at the bottom of the door had to be added on the mitred door, but can obviously be rebated in a frame-and-panel style door after due allowances are made"

veneer an MDF panel, and this gave rise to bookmatching opportunities.

Then, because this is laburnum, I could not resist inlaying a few oysters; of course this now very stable panel begged to be lipped, using mitres to good effect.

Clearly this is OTT, so I'll go into no further details other than to mention that the locating tongue at the bottom of the door had to be added on the mitred door, but can obviously be rebated in a frame-and-panel style door after due allowances are made.

Construction

I have given the exact sizes yielded by my example, *see dimensions drawing*, but these are not mandatory – although I do recommend that you start with a detailed full-scale drawing giving front and side elevations.

This is essential to work out drawer heights with their respective runner heights; it will also enable marking rods to be taken direct – time spent here will give rewards later.

Board up for the carcass, all the same section, and plan dovetails to cover the door location slot and for the grooves which take the back.

I don't do enough dovetailing to justify buying a jig but have a home-made device, *see photo 1*, for routing the tails, providing a neat edge for marking down for sockets.

I used my router to rough out the pins to finishing depth, *see photo 2*, then it's out with the chisels. The slots may be routed in at this stage.

"I was determined to design out many of the problems that I have witnessed"

Photo 3 Drawer guide slots are marked off using a rod to maintain accuracy

"It never ceases to amaze me how easy it is to make mistakes in this area, so spend plenty of time to avoid the dreaded wonky drawers' syndrome"

Guide slots

It never ceases to amaze me how easy it is to make mistakes in this area, so spend plenty of time setting up so as to avoid the dreaded wonky drawers' syndrome.

There are many ways of routing the slots and as I had a small batch, I assembled relevant side cheeks together against a straightedge, then, using a home-made sash-style clamp for the router to run against, I routed in the guide slots, *see photo 4*.

Immediately after slotting I added the runners which are glued to the front end of the slot for about 50mm (2in) and screwed

Because the catchplate can be fitted more easily before assembly, it's worth buying the lock and planning its final position. More importantly, the central pocket assembly actually covered part of mine.

The central dividing pocket is made next. Its four elements are jointed using through-dovetails which provide the strength for the sides to support the drawers. Notice also that this sub-assembly provides the stop against which the door comes to rest when shut.

A complete dry assembly with inner pocket in position now allows the drawer guide slots to be marked off using a rod, *see photo 3*, that being marked directly from the drawing.

Design solutions

During my years on the shop floor I have observed scores of wooden toolchests, from the cheapest to the dearest, so I was determined to design out many of the problems that I have witnessed.

Most common of these is collapse of the bottom drawer sides where the runners fail to take the weight of the contents.

Less common is that caused by chest backs being pushed off by drawers coming to an abrupt halt against them. Stopping drawers in this manner is not conventional, but let's not lose sight of the fact that we are building a toolbox here. Both these problems are mostly due to poor build so can easily be cured.

My design gives each drawer a different height. The offset pigeon hole dividing the upper section adds interest as well as accepting the classic engineers' handbook. Although most commercial chests seem to have comb-jointed drawers, with some comb joints in the carcass, I decided to dovetail throughout.

"I don't do enough dovetailing to justify buying a jig but have a home-made device for running in the tails, providing a neat edge for marking down for sockets"

▲ Photo 4 Using a home-made sash-style clamp for the router to run against and align all the slots perfectly, I routed in the guide slots

lightly to the back to allow for seasonal movement, *see photo 5*.

I felt no need to slot-screw here as there is no great width to the side cheeks; a slightly oversize hole for the screw should be forgiving enough.

While they were nicely exposed, I applied varnish to the inside faces of the pocket.

Gluing up can be done in stages; obviously the pocket first, then the pocket to the underside of the top, using screws as well as glue.

At final assembly the 6mm (¼in) back is glued and pinned into the side cheek grooves, followed by the insertion of a few screws through the back and into the pocket, to ensure a very strong carcass.

Drawers

Knobs – whether shop-bought or home-made – must be planned to maximise the depth of drawers. My example gives a 15mm (⅝in) gap between door and drawer front, the knobs being 14mm (⁹⁄₁₆in) deep.

Photo 5 Runners are glued in the front end of the slot and screwed to the back to allow for movement

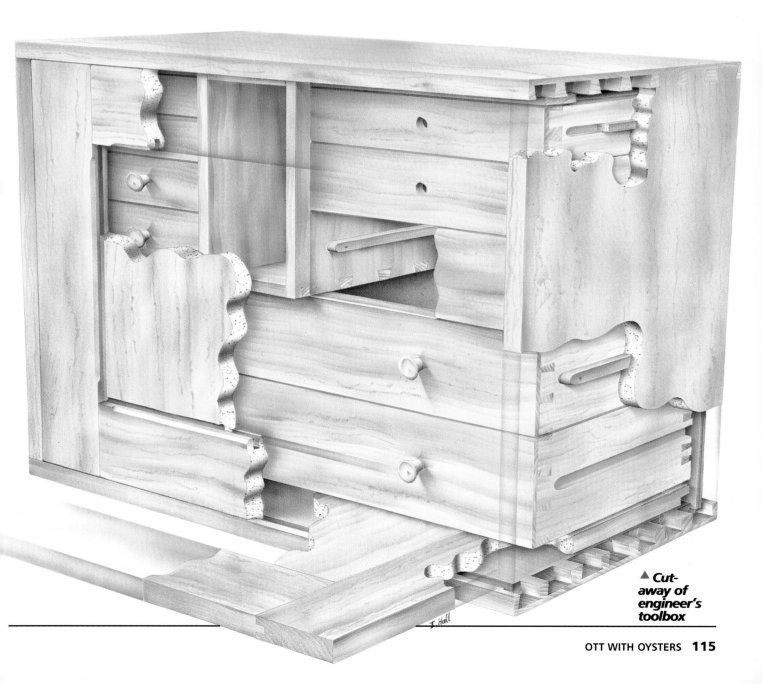

▲ Cut-away of engineer's toolbox

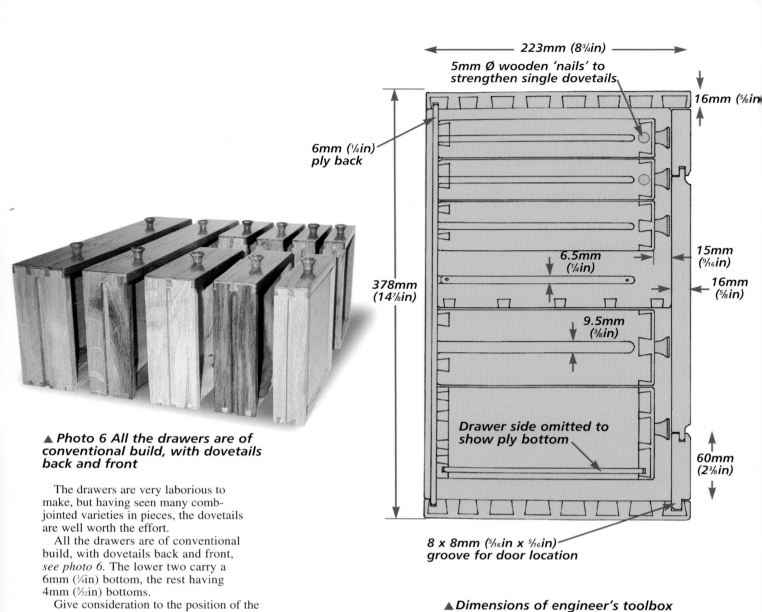

223mm (8¾in)

5mm Ø wooden 'nails' to strengthen single dovetails

16mm (⅝in)

6mm (¼in) ply back

378mm (14⅞in)

6.5mm (¼in)

15mm (⁹⁄₁₆in)

16mm (⅝in)

9.5mm (⅜in)

Drawer side omitted to show ply bottom

60mm (2⅜in)

8 x 8mm (⁵⁄₁₆in x ⁵⁄₁₆in) groove for door location

▲ **Photo 6 All the drawers are of conventional build, with dovetails back and front**

The drawers are very laborious to make, but having seen many comb-jointed varieties in pieces, the dovetails are well worth the effort.

All the drawers are of conventional build, with dovetails back and front, *see photo 6.* The lower two carry a 6mm (¼in) bottom, the rest having 4mm (⁵⁄₃₂in) bottoms.

Give consideration to the position of the runner slots as it is better that they don't pass through a joint at the back.

I used only one dovetail in the shallowest drawers, but this appeared to be weak so I added a dowel for insurance.

Another time-consuming operation is routing the runner slots. I planned the slots to pass through centres of drawer sides, but nonetheless set on a piece of scrap and fully check this in the chest before committing to the drawers.

With a batch of drawers to be created, getting well set up to produce the grooves on the router table is worthwhile, *see photo 7.*

▲**Dimensions of engineer's toolbox (Carcass side omitted for clarity)**

▼ **Photo 7 Set up to produce the grooves on the router table**

"Knobs – whether shop-bought or home-made – must be planned to maximise the depth of drawers"

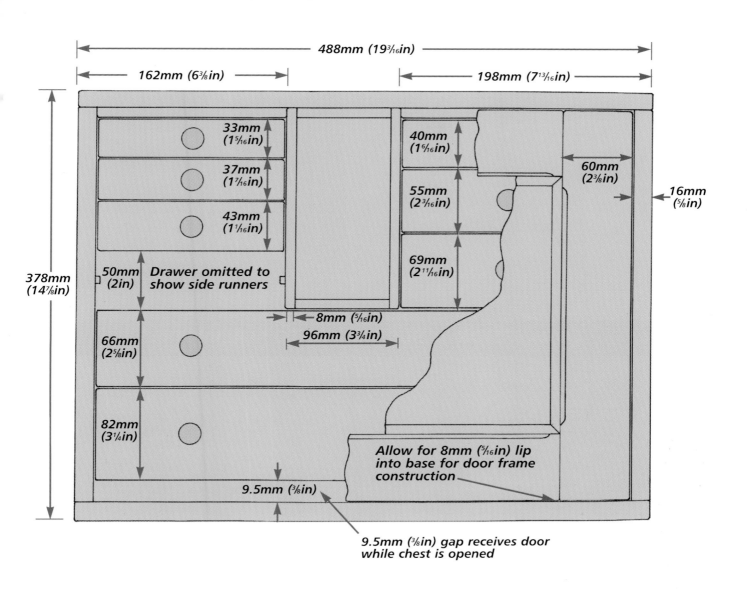

488mm (19³⁄₁₆in)

162mm (6⅜in)

198mm (7¹³⁄₁₆in)

33mm (1⁵⁄₁₆in)

37mm (1⁷⁄₁₆in)

43mm (1¹⁄₁₆in)

40mm (1⁶⁄₁₆in)

55mm (2³⁄₁₆in)

60mm (2⅜in)

16mm (⅝in)

69mm (2¹¹⁄₁₆in)

378mm (14⅞in)

50mm (2in)

Drawer omitted to show side runners

66mm (2⅝in)

8mm (⁵⁄₁₆in)

96mm (3¾in)

82mm (3¼in)

Allow for 8mm (⁵⁄₁₆in) lip into base for door frame construction

9.5mm (⅜in)

9.5mm (⅜in) gap receives door while chest is opened

▼ Completed engineer's toolbox

▶ A deviation to plan resulted in even more detail with laburnum oysters decorating the front panel

Door

The drawing shows the door that I intended to make before problems arose, *see above.*

Because the lock takes a sizeable 'bite' when fitting, the rails have to be fairly wide to prevent any weakness that might result.

The panels have endless possibilities. I've drawn a simple fielded one to the front, but flush to the back to provide a surface for when the chest is opened and the door is slipped beneath the bottom drawer.

Finish

Three or four coats of polyurethane varnish cut back finally with 0000 wirewool, and a lubrication with wax, were sufficient for the exterior of this piece.

A good internal waxing to achieve a smooth movement on drawers completes the task.

CONVERSION TABLE: INCHES TO MILLIMETRES

inch		mm	inch		mm	inch		mm
1/64	0.0565	0.3969	3/8	0.375	9.5250	47/64	0.734375	18.6531
1/32	0.03125	0.7938	25/64	0.390625	9.9219			
3/64	0.046875	1.1906	13/32	0.40625	10.3188	3/4	0.750	19.0500
1/16	0.0625	1.5875	27/64	0.421875	10.7156			
						49/64	0.765625	19.4469
5/64	0.078125	1.9844	7/16	0.4375	11.1125	25/32	0.78125	19.8438
3/32	0.09375	2.3812	29/64	0.453125	11.5094	51/64	0.796875	20.2406
7/64	0.109375	2.7781	15/32	0.46875	11.9062	13/16	0.8125	20.6375
			31/64	0.484375	12.3031			
1/8	0.125	3.1750				53/64	0.828125	21.0344
9/64	0.140625	3.5719	1/2	0.500	12.700	27/32	0.84375	21.0344
5/32	0.15625	3.9688	33/64	0.515625	13.0969	55/64	0.858375	21.8281
11/64	0.171875	4.3656	17/32	0.53125	13.4938			
			35/64	0.546875	13.8906	7/8	0.875	22.2250
3/16	0.1875	4.7625	9/16	0.5625	14.2875	57/64	0.890625	22.6219
13/64	0.203125	5.1594				29/32	0.90625	23.0188
7/32	0.21875	5.5562	37/64	0.578125	14.6844	59/64	0.921875	23.4156
15/64	0.234375	5.9531	19/32	0.59375	15.0812			
1/4	0.250	6.3500	39/64	0.609375	15.4781	15/16	0.9375	23.8125
						61/64	0.953125	24.2094
17/64	0.265625	6.7469	5/8	0.625	15.8750	31/32	0.96875	24.6062
9/32	0.28125	7.5406	41/64	0.640625	16.2719	63/64	0.984375	25.0031
5/16	0.3125	7.9375	21/32	0.65625	16.6688			
			43/64	0.671875	17.0656	1	1.00	25.4
21/64	0.1328125	8.3344	11/16	0.6875	17.4625			
11/32	0.34375	8.7312	45/64	0.703125	17.8594			
23/64	0.359375	9.1281	23/32	0.71875	18.2562			

index

GMC Publications

BOOKS

WOODCARVING

The Art of the Woodcarver	*GMC Publications*
Carving Architectural Detail in Wood: The Classical Tradition	
	Frederick Wilbur
Carving Birds & Beasts	*GMC Publications*
Carving the Human Figure: Studies in Wood and Stone	*Dick Onians*
Carving Nature: Wildlife Studies in Wood	*Frank Fox-Wilson*
Carving Realistic Birds	*David Tippey*
Decorative Woodcarving	*Jeremy Williams*
Elements of Woodcarving	*Chris Pye*
Essential Woodcarving Techniques	*Dick Onians*
Further Useful Tips for Woodcarvers	*GMC Publications*
Lettercarving in Wood: A Practical Course	*Chris Pye*
Making & Using Working Drawings for Realistic Model Animals	
	Basil F. Fordham
Power Tools for Woodcarving	*David Tippey*
Practical Tips for Turners & Carvers	*GMC Publications*
Relief Carving in Wood: A Practical Introduction	*Chris Pye*
Understanding Woodcarving	*GMC Publications*
Understanding Woodcarving in the Round	*GMC Publications*
Useful Techniques for Woodcarvers	*GMC Publications*
Wildfowl Carving – Volume 1	*Jim Pearce*
Wildfowl Carving – Volume 2	*Jim Pearce*
Woodcarving: A Complete Course	*Ron Butterfield*
Woodcarving: A Foundation Course	*Zoë Gertner*
Woodcarving for Beginners	*GMC Publications*
Woodcarving Tools & Equipment Test Reports	*GMC Publications*
Woodcarving Tools, Materials & Equipment	*Chris Pye*

WOODTURNING

Adventures in Woodturning	*David Springett*
Bert Marsh: Woodturner	*Bert Marsh*
Bowl Turning Techniques Masterclass	*Tony Boase*
Colouring Techniques for Woodturners	*Jan Sanders*
Contemporary Turned Wood: New Perspectives in a Rich Tradition	
	Ray Leier, Jan Peters & Kevin Wallace
The Craftsman Woodturner	*Peter Child*
Decorative Techniques for Woodturners	*Hilary Bowen*
Fun at the Lathe	*R.C. Bell*
Illustrated Woodturning Techniques	*John Hunnex*
Intermediate Woodturning Projects	*GMC Publications*
Keith Rowley's Woodturning Projects	*Keith Rowley*
Practical Tips for Turners & Carvers	*GMC Publications*
Turning Green Wood	*Michael O'Donnell*
Turning Miniatures in Wood	*John Sainsbury*
Turning Pens and Pencils	*Kip Christensen & Rex Burningham*
Understanding Woodturning	*Ann & Bob Phillips*
Useful Techniques for Woodturners	*GMC Publications*
Useful Woodturning Projects	*GMC Publications*
Woodturning: Bowls, Platters, Hollow Forms, Vases, Vessels, Bottles, Flasks, Tankards, Plates	*GMC Publications*
Woodturning: A Foundation Course (New Edition)	*Keith Rowley*
Woodturning: A Fresh Approach	*Robert Chapman*
Woodturning: An Individual Approach	*Dave Regester*
Woodturning: A Source Book of Shapes	*John Hunnex*
Woodturning Jewellery	*Hilary Bowen*
Woodturning Masterclass	*Tony Boase*
Woodturning Techniques	*GMC Publications*
Woodturning Tools & Equipment Test Reports	*GMC Publications*
Woodturning Wizardry	*David Springett*

WOODWORKING

Advanced Scrollsaw Projects	*GMC Publications*
Bird Boxes and Feeders for the Garden	*Dave Mackenzie*
Complete Woodfinishing	*Ian Hosker*
David Charlesworth's Furniture-Making Techniques	
	David Charlesworth
The Encyclopedia of Joint Making	*Terrie Noll*
Furniture & Cabinetmaking Projects	*GMC Publications*
Furniture-Making Projects for the Wood Craftsman	*GMC Publications*
Furniture-Making Techniques for the Wood Craftsman	
	GMC Publications
Furniture Projects	*Rod Wales*
Furniture Restoration (Practical Crafts)	*Kevin Jan Bonner*
Furniture Restoration and Repair for Beginners	*Kevin Jan Bonner*
Furniture Restoration Workshop	*Kevin Jan Bonner*
Green Woodwork	*Mike Abbott*
Kevin Ley's Furniture Projects	*Kevin Ley*
Making & Modifying Woodworking Tools	*Jim Kingshott*
Making Chairs and Tables	*GMC Publications*
Making Classic English Furniture	*Paul Richardson*
Making Little Boxes from Wood	*John Bennett*
Making Screw Threads in Wood	*Fred Holder*
Making Shaker Furniture	*Barry Jackson*
Making Woodwork Aids and Devices	*Robert Wearing*
Mastering the Router	*Ron Fox*
Minidrill: Fifteen Projects	*John Everett*
Pine Furniture Projects for the Home	*Dave Mackenzie*
Practical Scrollsaw Patterns	*John Everett*
Router Magic: Jigs, Fixtures and Tricks to Unleash your Router's Full Potential	*Bill Hylton*
Routing for Beginners	*Anthony Bailey*
The Scrollsaw: Twenty Projects	*John Everett*
Sharpening: The Complete Guide	*Jim Kingshott*
Sharpening Pocket Reference Book	*Jim Kingshott*
Simple Scrollsaw Projects	*GMC Publications*
Space-Saving Furniture Projects	*Dave Mackenzie*
Stickmaking: A Complete Course	*Andrew Jones & Clive George*
Stickmaking Handbook	*Andrew Jones & Clive George*
Test Reports: *The Router* and *Furniture & Cabinetmaking*	
	GMC Publications
Veneering: A Complete Course	*Ian Hosker*
Veneering Handbook	*Ian Hosker*
Woodfinishing Handbook (Practical Crafts)	*Ian Hosker*
Woodworking with the Router: Professional Router Techniques any Woodworker can Use	*Bill Hylton & Fred Matlack*
The Workshop	*Jim Kingshott*

TOYMAKING

Designing & Making Wooden Toys	*Terry Kelly*
Fun to Make Wooden Toys & Games	*Jeff & Jennie Loader*
Restoring Rocking Horses	*Clive Green & Anthony Dew*
Scrollsaw Toy Projects	*Ivor Carlyle*
Scrollsaw Toys for All Ages	*Ivor Carlyle*
Wooden Toy Projects	*GMC Publications*